TALK SEX

Sue Johanson is a registered nurse who has been a sex counsellor for nearly thirty years. She is the host of the "Sunday Night Sex Show," a weekly television programme, and her columns appear frequently in newspapers and magazines. A mother and grandmother, she speaks to thousands of teenagers in schools each year.

TALK SEX

Sue
Tells It Like It Is

SUE JOHANSON

Penguin Books

PENGUIN BOOKS
Published by the Penguin Group
Penguin Books Canada Ltd, 10 Alcorn Avenue, Toronto, Ontario,
Canada M4V 3B2
Penguin Books Ltd, 27 Wrights Lane, London W8 5TZ, England
Penguin Putnam Inc., 375 Hudson Street, New York, New York
10014, U.S.A.
Penguin Books Australia Ltd, Ringwood, Victoria, Australia
Penguin Books (NZ) Ltd, cnr Rosedale and Airborne Roads, Albany,
Auckland 1310, New Zealand

Penguin Books Ltd, Registered Offices: Harmondsworth, Middlesex, England

First published by Penguin Books Canada Limited, 1988

10 9 8 7 6 5 4

Copyright © Sue Johanson, 1988

Manufactured in Canada

Canadian Cataloguing in Publication Data
Johanson, Sue
Talk sex

ISBN 0-14-010377-5

1. Sex instruction for youth.   I. Title.

HQ35.J63 1988   306.7'088055   C87-094831-8

American Library of Congress Cataloguing in Publication Data Available

Visit Penguin Canada's web site at **www.penguin.ca**

*To my tribe, my children and grandchildren,
and to all the kids who have challenged me over the
years with their questions*

• ▲ • ▲ • ▲ • ▲ • ▲ • ▲ • ▲ • ▲ • ▲ • ▲ • ▲ • ▲ • ▲

Acknowledgments

I didn't do this alone. I had a lot of help from Catherine Yolles, Francine Geraci and Dr. Laurie Dempsey. I would like to thank Jeanette McLachlin, the AIDS Committee of Toronto, Beth Davey of the Birth Control and VD Information Centre, Janice Ristock, the Metro Action Committee of Public Violence Against Women & Children, the Canadian Cancer Society and the Sexual Assault Care Centre at Women's College Hospital. I would also like to thank everyone at Penguin for their enthusiasm and willingness to take the risk of publishing a book on sex for kids.

▪ ▲ ▪ ▲ ▪ ▲ ▪ ▲ ▪ ▲ ▪ ▲ ▪ ▲ ▪ ▲ ▪ ▲ ▪ ▲ ▪ ▲

Table of Contents

▲ • ▲ • ▲ • ▲ • ▲ • ▲ • ▲ • ▲ • ▲ • ▲ • ▲ • ▲ • ▲

Introduction

People often ask me how I got started as a sex counsellor. Until 1970, I was busy raising my three kids. Although I was trained as a nurse, I found I was not comfortable talking to my children about wet dreams, masturbation, birth control and sexually transmitted diseases.

When I started a teen birth-control clinic in 1970, I soon realized that I was not the only parent who found it difficult to talk to my own kids about sex. At that time, sex education in school consisted mostly of anatomy and physiology. (It still does in some areas.) The reason is that it's much easier to talk about sex this way. But teenagers don't care about Fallopian tubes and seminal vesicles; they want to know about love and feelings.

Schools began to invite me as a guest speaker to answer kids' questions about sex, and soon I was doing workshops for teachers and other professionals. I still do in-school presentations for about 30,000 kids a year.

In talking to teens this way I realized that many kids get their sex education from TV, radio and the newspapers. So I decided to make use of the media. The result was the "Sunday Night Sex Show with Sue" on Q107, a Toronto rock radio station, then a weekly

TV show, "Talking Sex with Sue." This led to a monthly column in *Chatelaine* magazine, and to this book.

I have based *Talk Sex* on actual written questions that kids have put into "Dear Sue" boxes in the schools I visit. The answers are specific and graphic—some parents may feel too much so. But kids want explicit answers to their questions on sexual activity, almost a "how-to" approach. So I try to tell it like it is. I feel we have pussyfooted around the topic of sex for too long. In this day and age, particularly with the new threat of AIDS, kids need specifics.

My attitudes, opinions and values do creep in. If I get a question from a fifteen-year-old—"How old should you be to have sex?"—I will say, "Fifteen is too young; you are just not ready. Wait till you are sure you have a loving, caring, committed relationship. At fifteen you may have galloping gonads, but by now you've learned you can't have everything you want when you want it. That's how it is with sex." This is my bias; you may or may not like it. But it comes from sixteen years of working with kids in my clinic.

I hope that parents will read this book and take every opportunity to discuss it with their kids. It's a perfect vehicle for teens and parents to share attitudes and values.

But this book was written for teens. It is *your* book about you and sex. You may find it best to start at the beginning and read right through to the end. Then you can go back and focus on your concerns.

So let's get on with the good stuff. . .

1

The Bod

For kids, being one of the gang is "Numero Uno" on everyone's list of priorities. Parents' opinions don't matter; teens are convinced that parents are fossils left over from the Stone Age. Your peers are the ones who count. Only they can provide the three big A's necessary for survival—Acceptance, Approval and Appreciation.

While nobody wants to be different, we are all searching for a way to express our own uniqueness and individuality. Yet we must find it within the confines of what our particular group or gang finds acceptable.

This need to look, act and feel like everybody else puts a lot of pressure on teens, pressure that is evident in your letters and calls to my radio and TV shows. Some of your more common concerns are reflected in the questions included in this chapter.

My ultimate goal is to reassure you that almost everything falls within the range of "normal." There is very little that is truly abnormal. But most males are convinced that they have the smallest penis in the whole school, and most females believe they are terminally flat chested and have thunder thighs. Is there anything I can say to dispute the logic of self-doubt?

You *will* survive your teenage years. Reassurances

that you are not "zit city"; that your body is great and wonderful will probably fall on deaf ears. But it's worth a try.

Males

Let's take a quick look at your bod:

Penis. (Slang terms are cock, prick, dick, rod, tool, or weenie.) The penis has two parts, the head (or glans) and the shaft. The penis is made up of spongy tissue loaded with blood vessels. When a male is "turned on," or sexually aroused, these fill with blood, causing the penis to swell, grow rigid and erect—also known as "getting a hard-on" or "popping a boner" (although there is no bone in the penis).

The glans of an uncircumcised penis is covered by a thick fold of retractable skin called the foreskin. This serves as a protective hood for the glans, which contains many nerve endings and is highly sensitive. A white, waxy secretion called smegma collects under the foreskin. A male should wash it away regularly to prevent irritation and infection.

Testicles (or testes). (Slang terms are balls, nuts, plunkers, rocks, jewels or bangers.) These are two organs, each the size of a walnut, suspended in a darkish, crinkly sac of skin called the scrotum. One testicle usually hangs lower than the other (which probably makes walking a lot more comfortable). The scrotum is sensitive to touch and temperature, hangs lower in hot weather to allow more skin surface for perspiration to evaporate, and pulls up closer to the body when a male is cold, nervous or sexually aroused. At puberty, the testicles begin to produce sperm and the hormone testosterone. This is the hormone which triggers the other physical changes we associate with growing up male.

Epididymis. A single long, thin tube, bunched up in each testicle. This is where sperm is stored till a male becomes sexually aroused. When that happens, the sperm is forced into the vas deferens.

Vas deferens. (Also called seminal ducts or vas.) Two narrow tubes that carry sperm to the point where it mixes with the other fluids that together make up semen, the fluid that is expelled from the penis when a male reaches the peak of sexual arousal and ejaculates ("cums").

Prostate. A gland located just below the urinary bladder. It produces seminal fluid, the milky liquid that transports and nourishes sperm.

Cowper's glands. Two glands located below the prostate. During sexual arousal, but before ejaculation, they secrete a small amount of fluid, which appears at the tip of the penis. This fluid, which is for lubrication, contains sperm and can cause pregnancy.

Semen. (Slang terms are cum, spunk, jism.) Semen is the sperm, plus seminal fluid that is expelled in spurts from the tip of the penis when a male ejaculates. There may be three to eight such spurts, releasing a total of about a tablespoon of thick, whitish, creamy fluid. While only about a quarter of this is sperm, the average ejaculation contains approximately 360 million of them, enough to re-populate

North America in one shot! There are billions of sperm stored in a male's testicles at all times. Each one has a limited life-span. Then they break down, to be absorbed by the system and replaced by new sperm. Although frequent ejaculation may slightly reduce the concentration of sperm, there is absolutely no chance of using them up. So relax, guys— there's lots more where that came from.

Urethra.   A narrow tube running through the penis. It is connected to the seminal vesicle and to the bladder, and carries urine as well as semen, but not at the same time. When the penis becomes erect, a valve in the urethra closes the passage to the bladder, which is why a male can't urinate when he has an erection. After ejaculation (or whenever the erection subsides), it takes a few moments for this valve to relax again, allowing him to urinate.

•　▲　•

What is the normal size of a penis?

This is a question I'm always asked. Most guys are preoccupied with the size of their penis, and are usually convinced that theirs is the smallest in the whole school.

Almost all males experience a growth spurt at some point during puberty, and by the age of seventeen or eighteen the penis will have reached its full adult size. The average non-erect adult penis measures anywhere between two to four inches. When erect, it may be from four to eight inches long and one to two inches in diameter. There is nothing you can do to speed up the growth process and once you have stopped growing there is nothing you can do to make your penis bigger.

Knowing this may not seem like much help. But regardless of the myths that "bigger is better," penis size is not important for sexual satisfaction for males or females. Nor will it affect your ability to have children.

• ▲ •

I've heard that you either use it or lose it. Does this mean that unless I have sex soon I won't be able to do it later?

A common misconception among males is that the penis is a "love muscle," and if you don't exercise it regularly, it will shrivel up or forget what it's supposed to do.

No way! Even if you've never had sex before, or maybe it's just been a while since you've done it, your body will know exactly what to do when the time comes. You'd be amazed at how naturally and instinctively the bod reacts and responds.

• ▲ •

One night about three weeks ago I think I wet the bed. My mother didn't say anything, and I didn't think any more about it, but then it happened again last night. I'm twelve years old, and haven't done this since I was a baby. What's the matter?

Are you sure it was urine? It sounds to me like you had your first wet dream.

A male's first ejaculation of semen usually comes about a year after his penis and testicles have started to grow noticeably, at about the same time as his growth spurt in height. He will probably also have some armpit and pubic hair. If he does not have his first ejaculation while touching his genitals (playing with himself, or masturbating) he will probably do so during what is called a nocturnal emission—a release of semen that occurs while he is asleep. Because nocturnal emissions often happen while you are dreaming a nice, sexy dream (although you may not remember it the next day), they are called wet dreams. They are perfectly normal and natural; both males and females have them, and although females don't ejaculate, they do become sexually aroused and their genitals become lubricated. Amazing, isn't it—all this happens and you may sleep right through it!

Mom probably knows what's going on but may be uncomfortable talking about it. In any case, please don't feel worried or guilty about having wet dreams; they're nature's way of releasing sexual tension.

• ▲ •

One of my testicles hangs lower than the other and is a bit larger. Does this mean something?

Yes. It means you are completely normal. In most males the left testicle hangs lower than the right, though this is not always the case. If the two hung perfectly side by side, they'd be banging into each other with the slightest movement—not very comfortable, and potentially injurious to these delicate reproductive organs. As far as size goes, our bodies are never perfectly symmetrical. In most of us, one hand, one foot or one ear will be a bit larger than the other. Testicles are no exception.

• ▲ •

I have three testicles. How is this possible?

While it's possible to have three testicles, it is highly unlikely. More probably you have a varicocele (a ballooning of a blood vessel), or perhaps a hernia where part of the bowel has slid into the scrotal sac. In any case, you should check it out with a doctor as soon as possible.

• ▲ •

What are blue balls?

In a word—pain. When a male is sexually aroused, the blood supply to his genitals increases, and the resulting congestion may not completely subside unless he ejaculates. If arousal without ejaculation occurs not just once but frequently, the testicles feel hot, heavy and begin to throb. The resulting discomfort and irritability may stem more from feelings of frustration. The testicles actually take on a slightly bluish color—hence the name "blue balls," also know as "lover's nuts."

Most males masturbate before they reach this point, and that's probably the best way to ease the discomfort.

• ▲ •

The other day I was playing soccer and forgot my jock strap and got kneed in the nuts. It really hurt. That night my balls turned all black and blue. Will I be damaged for life? Will my voice go way up high? Will I be able to have kids?

None of that will happen. You got bashed and bruised and you'll be sore for a week or so, but you'll be fine. If the pain does last for more than two weeks, then get it checked out.

• ▲ •

Lately I have been having a big *problem. It doesn't matter where I am, eating in the cafeteria, talking to a girl, or concentrating on a math exam, when all of a sudden—POW! A monster hard-on. It's embarrassing. Does it mean I'm oversexed?*

What you are having is a spontaneous erection, and all males get them. A newborn baby boy may get his first spontaneous erection within five minutes after delivery, and may continue to experience them throughout his life. Spontaneous erections are generally most frequent around puberty and seem always to occur in the wrong place and at the wrong time. There you are, on the starting block the day of the big swim race, all ready to dive in, and. . . . You guessed it. You look down at your bulging crotch and moan, "Not now, you turkey!" Or, you finally get up the nerve to ask a girl to dance. It's a slow dance, and there you are—with this bulge in your blue jeans.

While these situations are uncomfortable and embarrassing, they're also perfectly normal and natural. They do not mean that you have too many hormones or are oversexed or perverted. The best thing to do when you have an erection in public is to cover it—with your raincoat, some books, anything—and try to think of something else. It will soon subside on its own. And nobody ever died, or exploded, or went crazy, because of an unfulfilled erection.

Females need to understand spontaneous erections,

too. If you're dancing with a guy and all of a sudden he acts embarrassed, don't leap to the assumption that you are in imminent danger of sexual assault. Just suggest you stop and have a pop, and be cool.

Spontaneous erections usually continue until a male reaches his early twenties. By the time he's thirty, he may wish they would happen again!

• ▲ •

I felt a lump in my testicle. What should I do?

You should see your family doctor as soon as possible. It may not be serious, but you should have it looked at. I'm glad you recognized the importance of checking your testicles. It's something you should do every time you're lathering up in the shower.

• ▲ •

What is an undescended testicle? Is it serious? What can be done about it?

Testicles form inside the abdomen of the male fetus and stay there until about the seventh month of pregnancy. At that time they descend into the scrotal sac through an opening called the inguinal canal. Then the canal closes to prevent a loop of bowel from descending, too.

Occasionally a boy is born with one or both of his testicles still up in his abdomen. Called undescended testicles, they usually fall into place on their own within a few months. If they have not gone down by the time a male is two years old, a doctor will perform a simple operation, under general anaesthetic, to pop the testicles into the scrotum and close the inguinal canal, which prevents their return to the abdomen. If the testicles remain in the abdomen there is the possibility of permanent sterility so it's important to have the condition treated by a doctor.

• ▲ •

I am fifteen and a half years old. Sometimes my friends and I watch porn videos. In one, we saw this guy whose penis curved to one side, and all my friends were laughing and joking about it. I felt uncomfortable because mine curves to the right when I have a hard-on. Is this caused by masturbation? (I use my right hand.) Is there an operation to straighten it out? I don't want my parents to know.

This condition, which is fairly common, has absolutely nothing to do with masturbation, much less which hand you use. There are two kinds of curvatures of the penis. In the most common, called chordee, the cord at the base of the penis is a little too tight and pulls the penis to one side. Unless the curvature is severe, it does not affect sexual performance or satisfaction and does not require treatment. The other condition, Peyronie's Disease, occurs mostly in older males. A dense, fibrous mass develops in the penis, preventing it from becoming fully engorged with blood during erection. The penis then curves to one side, making erection and penetration painful.

See your doctor for a diagnosis. The doctor will check that your penis hangs normally when not erect, and will ask you a few important questions: whether your penis curves with masturbation, whether erection and ejaculation are painful to you, and whether such discomfort keeps you from having sex. Since all consultations with your doctor are confidential, your parents need not know.

• ▲ •

When I have sex I get this dull, aching pain in my groin. What could be wrong?

Any number of things. You could have an infection in your bladder, prostate or one of your testicles. One testicle might be twisted or have a varicose vein (varicocele). Do make an appointment with your doctor immediately. The doctor will take samples of your blood and urine, and check for any growths, a hernia, a varicocele, or anything else.

Males occasionally experience pain during sex from stress or anxiety. But if it happens regularly, see your doctor.

• ▲ •

What is meant by the expression "dressing to the left" or "dressing to the right"?

Males develop the habit, when getting dressed, of tucking the penis either to the left or to the right side of their underwear. If you have a suit tailor-made, the tailor will want to know whether you dress left or right, and will allow a little extra room on the appropriate side for the bulge!

• ▲ •

What is circumcision?

Circumcision is the surgical removal of the foreskin of the penis. It is usually performed on a baby a few days after birth for religious or cultural reasons.

•　▲　•

I wasn't circumcised when I was born. Lately, I've had trouble pulling back the foreskin of my penis to wash. It's also uncomfortable when I have sex. Can I be circumcised safely at my age? I'm seventeen.

Adult circumcision is occasionally performed in cases of phimosis, a condition where the foreskin is so tight that it interferes with erection, and sometimes urination. But it may not be necessary to remove the foreskin completely. Many doctors today prefer a procedure known as a dorsal slit: a small incision about one-half inch, is made at the end of the foreskin and allows easier retraction.

Your family doctor can refer you to a urologist who will assess your particular situation.

•　▲　•

I am a seventeen-year-old guy, and when I neck with my girl-friend, my nipples get hard and poky. Is this normal?

Great question! Yes, it's perfectly normal. In both males and females, the breasts are an erogenous zone— a part of your body that feels great when touched. We pay more attention to female breasts, probably because they're larger and more obvious. But males and females possess the same nerve endings in their breasts, and so the nipples react similarly to stimulation. Touching your partner's breasts and nipples can be a tender and erotic gesture, whichever sex you are.

Another similarity: because males have a small amount of breast tissue, they may also develop breast cancer, and although it's more common in females, it's still a good idea, once a month, when you are in the shower lathering up, to examine the area around your nipples for any lumps and bumps as described on page 22/23.

• ▲ •

Help! I'm a twelve-year old guy, and I think I'm beginning to grow breasts. I'm too embarrassed to wear a T-shirt, and the guys in the locker room call me Bazooms.

Occasionally a male baby may be born with small breasts. The condition usually subsides within a few weeks after birth.

All males have a small amount of female sex hormones in their systems, just as females have a small amount of male hormones. A slight variation may cause some males to develop breasts around the onset of puberty. These males may also tend to be slightly overweight.

Being teased hurts—especially when it's your body being laughed at. Puberty is tough enough without being teased about "looking like a girl."

The good news is your breasts will probably flatten

out as your male hormones take over. But if this problem continues into your twenties and really bothers you, ask your family doctor to do a hormone profile on you. As a last resort, your breasts can be reduced surgically.

Meanwhile, you can be in style with great sloppy T-shirts and sweats. The only way to cope with the guys in the locker room is to ignore them. But it is rough.

Females

There are many slang words for female genitals—pussy, snatch, muff, or twat. Since most females are not comfortable with their genitals I would encourage any female who has never taken a good look at her genitals to take a mirror and identify the visible parts.

Labia.   The first thing you will see, under the pubic hair, are the labia majora, or large lips. They are much like the lips on your mouth—skin on the outside, mucous membranes on the inside. Their spongy, fatty tissue folds over to protect the inner genitals.

If you separate the labia major, you will find the labia minora, which are thinner, inner lips, and have mucous membranes on both sides. There are many nerve endings here that are easily stimulated by touch. When a female is sexually aroused, the labia become engorged with blood, they become swollen and turn a darker red.

Clitoris.   This small, round, firm, pea-shaped organ is located inside the labia at the top. Loaded with nerve endings, the clitoris has one function only— sexual arousal. Normally the clitoris hides in the upper folds of the labia minora, but when a female is sexually aroused, it becomes erect and protrudes much like a male's penis. When the stimulation ceases, it retracts again.

Hymen. Sometimes known as the cherry, the hymen is a thin membrane that partially covers the vaginal opening. It has one or more openings to allow menstrual blood to flow through. With sexual intercourse, this membrane stretches to allow entry of the penis into the vagina. Not every female is born with a hymen. And often, it is stretched or ruptured long before a female has sexual intercourse—by inserting tampons, for example, or by engaging in active sports.

Vagina. It extends upward and inward from the labia minora as a tube-like passage three to five inches long. The vagina is lined with mucous membrane, all wrinkled and folded so that it can expand. And expand it does, large enough to allow an eight-pound baby to pass through. It can also accommodate any size penis; it relaxes and lengthens to admit a large one, contracts and tightens to fit snugly around a small one.

When a female is sexually aroused, the vaginal walls are stimulated and produce lubrication. This clear, slippery fluid makes intercourse more comfortable and pleasurable for both partners. Also during arousal, the vagina changes shape, ballooning out at the top and tightening around the opening, to gently contain the penis during intercourse and to hold in the sperm.

The bottom third of the vagina contains many nerve endings and is highly sensitive to sexual stimulation, while the top two-thirds have few nerve endings. For this reason, most females feel little discomfort while undergoing an internal pelvic examination by a doctor.

Unlike a male—most of the female reproductive system is "internal" and so is not visible. But it is there!

Uterus (or womb). This hollow organ is the chamber where a baby develops during pregnancy. Looking much like an upside-down pear, it has dense, elastic walls capable of expanding to four times their original size. The uterus sheds its soft, spongy lining each month if it is not needed to cushion and nourish a developing baby. This process, known as menstruation (often called a period), generally lasts about five days, after which a new lining is built up all over again.

The top of the uterus is called the fundus, the centre is called the body, and the base is the cervix. A female can feel her cervix by inserting two fingers (make sure they're clean!) into the vagina and very gently pressing up and back. The round knob, with its little dimple in the centre, is the cervix. It has an opening (os) through which menstrual flow passes.

Ovaries. There are two of these, each located about three inches from each side of the belly button and slightly below it. About the size and shape of an almond, the ovaries do not function until puberty. Then they begin to produce two female hormones, estrogen and progesterone, triggering the changes associated with puberty—pubic and armpit hair as well as breast development. The ovaries also contain eggs (ova)—many thousands of them. Each ovum waits in its own capsule (follicle) until its time to ripen. After puberty, one egg per month ripens, pops out of its follicle and is picked up by the adjacent Fallopian tube. This process is known as ovulation.

Ovulation continues until the female is about forty-five to fifty-five years of age. Then it stops. This is known as menopause.

Fallopian tubes.　　Lying just above the ovaries and connected directly to the uterus, these tubes are about three inches long and about as thick as the lead in a pencil. Conception—the union of an egg and sperm—always takes place in one of the Fallopian tubes, never in the uterus. The fertilized egg is propelled along in a wavelike motion, by the tiny fine hairs that line the tube, to the uterus. This takes from three to six days. The fertilized egg then implants itself in the lining of the uterus, where it grows and receives nourishment through a mass of blood vessels called the placenta. Shortly after the birth of the baby, the placenta is expelled.

• ▲ •

I am thirteen years old and flat as a board. All my friends have boobs. Is this normal?

Once you have entered puberty and a certain proportion of your body is fat, then you will start to develop breasts. This may occur as early as age nine or as late as sixteen. Heredity is a big factor; you may come from a family of late bloomers.

When your breasts do develop, you will notice some changes in the nipples. They become larger, pinker or darker and develop fine pale yellow bumps, called Montgomery nodes. These are perfectly normal, so don't worry—it's okay.

A lot of emphasis is placed on females' breasts, but this is just one indication of puberty. There are many others. Have your hips flared out? Have you got armpit and pubic hair? Has menstruation started? If nothing has happened by the time you are eighteen, ask your doctor to do a hormone profile for you.

•   ▲   •

One of my breasts is larger than the other. Is this normal?

Yes, very. No body is perfectly symmetrical. Chances are one of your hands is larger than the other, and I doubt that both your feet are exactly the same size.

If you truly feel self-conscious, you might add a bit of stuffing to your bra on your small side. But if the difference is slight, no one will notice. You're probably more aware of it than anyone else.

•   ▲   •

If I squeeze my nipple, I get a thick, whitish-yellow discharge from my breast. What is this? I have never been pregnant.

Any breast discharge that does not occur during or right after pregnancy is cause for concern. This condition is called galactorrhoea and generally signals a hormonal imbalance, and should therefore be checked immediately by your doctor.

•   ▲   •

My boobs are so small. I just hate the way I look and I don't feel female.

Unfortunately many people equate femininity and sex appeal with having noticeable breasts. But you are female no matter how big or small your breasts may be. I can promise you that the girl who you think has magnificent breasts is convinced they're too big and wishes hers were more like yours.

Perhaps your breasts aren't fully developed yet. Until they are you can give mother nature a helping hand. Buy bras with a fibre-fill liner. These are comfortable and subtle. Or you can buy foam falsies that slip inside your bra. There is nothing you can do to increase your breast size—no creams, pills, or exercises. Surgery can be performed to implant small bags of silicone (a jelly-like substance) under the skin of your breasts, but this operation would not be performed until you are over twenty years old.

Would it help you to know that every female has the same number of nerve endings in her breasts. Females with large breasts have more area to cover so the sensations are not as strong. Think positive!

• ▲ •

I have humungous breasts. I have to wear a heavy-duty bra and the straps dig into my shoulders. I'm sick and tired of guys at school trying to cop a feel.

Some kids really are uncomfortable and embarrassed because they have large breasts which hinder involvement in sports, dancing—almost everything you do. And being top-heavy can definitely affect your body image and sense of self-esteem. The weight of your breasts may cause you to be round shouldered and experience back pain. Clothing can also be a problem. Nobody wants to live in oversize T-shirts all the time.

Explain your feelings to your parents. Tell them you would like to see your family doctor who will discuss the possibility of breast reduction surgery. The surgery may result in some scarring and reduction in sensation. Breastfeeding may also be a problem in the future, so talk about this with your doctor.

Guys are another problem. Some guys feel that females with large breasts are really sexy numbers and assume they must be interested in sex. So you have to develop the ability to say "Get lost!" loud and clear until they get the message.

I know it is small comfort right now, but it will get easier as you get older and more confident about yourself.

• ▲ •

Just before my period begins, my breasts get so uncomfortable, tender and large. Is there anything I can do?

This is very common. Just prior to menstruation, your hormones change their balance, fluid collects in the tissues, and the breasts feel heavy, bulgy and sore. Try cutting down on your intake of salt and fluids for a few days before your period, and eat foods rich in B-vitamins—whole-grain cereals, liver—and potassium and vitamin C—leafy greens, fresh fruits. This may help to make you more comfortable. In any case, you'll be back to normal in two or three days.

• ▲ •

I have lots of little lumps in my breasts. Is this normal, or should I worry about cancer?

All unusual lumps should be checked by your doctor. But it sounds as though you may have what are called "ropy," or cystic, breasts, a harmless condition where small, fibrous lumps come and go.

If you check your breasts every month as described on page 22/23, you'll be alert to any changes from what is normal for you, and you can tell your family doctor about them.

• ▲ •

I think my nipples are too small. Sometimes they shrivel up entirely. This embarrasses me when changing in front of the girls in my swimming class.

Nipples vary in size, colour and shape for every female. Poky erect nipples, broad flat nipples, even inverted nipples—all are normal, attractive and sexy, will transmit pleasurable erotic sensations, and when the time comes, will function equally well for breastfeeding.

The darker, brownish-pink area around the nipple, called the areola, has small bumps on it naturally. A few hairs sometimes grow on the skin around the areola. The shrivelling you mention is caused by the nerve endings in the nipple, which make it highly sensitive. Your nipples will pucker and become erect when you are sexually aroused, but also when you're cold and wet—which is probably what happens in swim class.

So, for all you guys who think erect nipples mean you've really turned her on—sorry, it ain't necessarily so.

• ▲ •

You're always talking about breast self examination. How do you do it?

Breast Self-Examination

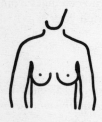

1. Sit or stand in front of your mirror, with your arms relaxed at your sides, and examine your breasts for any changes in size and shape. Look for any puckering or dimpling of the skin, and for any discharge or change in the nipples.

2. Then, raise both your arms over your head, and look for exactly the same things.

3. Lie on your bed, with your left hand under your head. Starting at the outside of your breast, near your armpit, and with the fingers of your right hand held together flat, press gently but firmly with small circular motions to feel the breast tissue between your fingers and your chest wall. Check for unusual lumps or changes.

4. Now move your fingers in toward the nipple about 2 cms and feel all the way around again. Repeat this action as many times as necessary to be sure you have covered the entire breast, including the nipple.

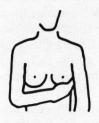

5. Now bring your left arm down to your side and still using the flat part of your fingers, feel under your armpit, since breast tissue is found there as well.

6. Repeat the entire procedure using your left hand on your right breast.

Examine your breasts every month—a few days after your period ends is best.

If you find any change in your breast, check it out with your doctor right away. Don't be frightened—most breast lumps or changes are not cancer, but why take the chance?

I have some dark hair around my nipples, the top of my legs and down my stomach. Is there anything I can do?

Although you may feel like Godzilla the gorilla, everyone's got body hair, and many females are just as embarrassed by it as you are. Heredity is a factor—if your parents have a fair bit of body hair, you probably will too.

Females who have unwanted body hair can have electrolysis—a process in which a tiny needle is inserted into the hair follicle (the tiny sac that contains the hair root), and a small electric current is sent through the needle, killing the root. The procedure may have to be repeated because it is hard to zap all the hairs at one time, but a few months of weekly treatments can weed them out. Electrolysis must be done by a licensed practitioner and it is generally not covered by government health plans. The price depends on the size of the area to be covered. Talk to your mom and dad, and family doctor about it.

Occasionally too much hair growth signifies a hormonal problem which can be assessed by your doctor.

Plucking, tweezing, shaving and waxing are temporary measures. None are harmful and they will not make the hair grow back thicker. You can also bleach facial and body hair to make it look lighter, but bleach should not be used near the genitals. Use only a facial-quality bleach obtained from a cosmetician at a drug store. Do not try to concoct your own; you could burn yourself.

Males also can find excess body hair embarrassing and frustrating. In their case, there isn't much that can

be done about it. Fortunately, many females like nothing better than to run their fingers through a guy's
thick, soft, fuzzy hair.

• ▲ •

*My genitals are so ugly—the labia are darker and
bigger than I think they should be.*

The key word in your letter is "should." Who says
genitals *should* look one way or another? And how
many sets of female genitals have you examined?

I hope you aren't comparing your genitals with those
you might see in skin magazines where the photographs
of the models' bodies, including their genitals, are often
touched up for cosmetic appeal. In any case, all genitals
look slightly different, and none are ugly.

Most females aren't aware that males find dark,
dusky labia a real turn-on, because they're a signal that
a female is sexually aroused and receptive. If these
qualities are yours naturally, you've got it made! Your
partner will appreciate every pucker and fold.

• ▲ •

*Sometimes I get this yucky discharge from my vagina.
It smells. Does every girl have this? Will douching
help?*

Normally, vaginal secretions keep the vagina clean.
After menstruation, the discharge is thick, white and
waxy; at ovulation, it becomes clear and stringy like
raw egg white. These fluids keep the vagina slightly acid

and control normal micro-organisms. Normal vaginal discharge has a distinctive odour that many males find sexually stimulating.

Douching—introducing warm water, or a store-bought mixture, into the vagina—is not recommended. It washes away the vagina's natural protective fluids, making it more vulnerable to infection.

Occasionally, when you've been under stress, or taking antibiotics, the normal balance of micro-organisms in the vagina may get out of whack, and you may find yourself with vaginitis, a broad term that covers a variety of symptoms such as increased discharge, which causes itching, burning, swelling and redness. If you have any of these symptoms, get your buns to the doctor quickly; it's also possible you have a sexually transmitted disease (see chapter 5). But what you've described is probably very normal, and yes, every female does have it.

•   ▲   •

I am nineteen and do not have a boyfriend. Should I have a pelvic exam every year even though I'm not into sex? What will happen when the doctor examines me?

All women between the ages of eighteen and sixty-five whether or not they are sexually active, should have a Pap smear—a test for early signs of cancer—once a year. The doctor should examine your breasts for lumps and bumps at the same time. But if you're younger than eighteen and are having sex you should have a yearly exam starting *now*.

During a pelvic exam, also called an internal or bi-manual exam, the physician checks your external genitals, vagina and rectum.

Now, here's what happens at the doctor's office.

When you go into the examination room, the doctor or a nurse asks you to take off your clothes, including bra and panties and hands you a gown to put on. Then you are left alone to change.

The doctor returns and asks you to lie on the examination table, and a sheet is draped over your abdomen. Some doctors have foot-rests or "stirrups" on either side of the examination table; others ask the patient to place her heels together and flop her legs open, which is really more comfortable. The doctor then shines a light on the genitals, checking to make sure there are no infections and nothing unusual. The rectum is examined for herpes, warts, hemorrhoids or discharge.

If the genitals are irritated or swollen, the doctor will want to test for infections, along with the routine Pap smear and test for gonorrhea. These tests require a sample smear of cervical secretions. The doctor very gently inserts a plastic or metal speculum, an instrument that gently holds apart the vaginal walls, into the vagina in order to see the cervix. (This doesn't hurt, but it does feel strange, because we normally don't walk around with a speculum stuck in our vagina!) Looking for discharge or unusual bumps that might indicate an infection, the doctor touches the cervix lightly with a long cotton swab to pick up some of the secretions, but you won't feel it.

Finally, the doctor removes the speculum, puts on a thin plastic glove, inserts two gloved fingers into the vagina and presses gently upward, just behind the cervix, while the other hand presses down on the abdomen, just above the pubic bone. Now the doctor is checking the ovaries and uterus for tumors or cysts, and to rule out pregnancy. After this is done, that's it. It's over.

Once the doctor leaves the room, you get dressed. The whole process takes about ten minutes. A pelvic exam is simple, and it's good, preventative medicine.

Before you leave the doctor's office, if you need birth control, now is the time to talk about it.

If you're embarrassed to go to the family doctor who has known you since you were a baby, then find another. You may feel more comfortable with a female doctor; some male doctors, anticipating that their female patients might be uncomfortable, will have a female nurse in the room during the pelvic examination. In any case, most family doctors do on average ten pelvic exams a day. Don't be embarrassed. They've seen it all, so unless your genitals light up, smile or wink, they are just like everybody else's.

• ▲ •

Do girls ovulate every month?

Not necessarily. You don't ovulate when you're pregnant. Stress can also cause you to miss a month or ovulate at an unusual time. Women over thirty often don't necessarily ovulate every month, which makes getting pregnant—conception—more difficult for them. When a woman does not ovulate at all, the condition is known as sterility, and means she can't have children. But medication is available that can trigger ovulation in some infertile women.

• ▲ •

How do you know when you're ovulating? Can ovulation be felt?

A female who menstruates regularly is probably ovulating. If she has sex without birth control, she can get pregnant.

At ovulation, the vaginal secretions turn from white and waxy to clear and stringy. Some females claim they can feel when they ovulate—the ovum popping out of the ovary may cause a slight twinge or pulling sensation on one side or the other. If this happens and your calendar says you're mid-cycle, it probably was ovulation.

• ▲ •

How come you get your first period, then it takes ages for it to come again and you never know when it is coming?

When a female first begins menstruating, her cycle may not follow a regular, predictable, 28-day pattern. She might have one period, then wait four months for the next; the third might come after six weeks or three months. But as her hormone balance becomes established, her cycle will settle into a more-or-less regular pattern, ranging from 25 to 32 days between periods.

• ▲ •

Is there any danger of toxic shock syndrome from using tampons?

Toxic shock syndrome is a rare condition. It occurs when bacteria build up and are contained in the vagina, causing nausea, vomiting, diarrhea, fever and a sharp drop in blood pressure. It is not necessarily tampon-related—it occurs occasionally in females who do not use tampons, and also in males.

Still, it is possible that the use of a tampon could allow bacteria to build up and not escape. So in order to prevent toxic shock syndrome, it is recommended that you change your tampon every four hours and use a sanitary pad at night. If you get into the habit of never leaving a tampon in for more than four hours, you will be fine.

• ▲ •

I want to use tampons but I can't insert one. What should I do?

Believe me, most of us have fumbled and failed the first few times we tried to use tampons. But once you've got the knack, it's easy. Here are step by step instructions:

- Buy the smallest tampons available, not the super absorbent kind.
- Read the instructions provided in the package.
- Apply a small amount of petroleum jelly to the top of a tampon and around the sides of the applicator. This will make the tampon easier to insert.
- Then, while sitting on the toilet, or standing with one foot on the toilet seat (whichever way is most comfortable for you), find the opening to the vagina. It's okay to touch your genitals—you won't hurt yourself. Then gently insert the tampon into the vagina toward the small of your back. If you're having difficulty, slightly change

the angle of the tampon and try again. Once the tampon is inserted you shouldn't feel it at all.

- To remove the tampon sit on the toilet, reach around, find the string and gently pull to remove. Now you're ready to insert another.

- Change the tampon every four hours. You should not leave one in overnight because of the risk of toxic shock syndrome. Use a sanitary pad at night instead.

There! It was easy! But if after several attempts you are still unable to use a tampon you should see your doctor.

• ▲ •

Is there any way you can lose the tampon?

No, it has nowhere to go, so it will remain in the vagina. If you can't find the string, simply insert two fingers into the vagina—no harm done—and gently grasp the tampon and remove it.

• ▲ •

Is it okay to have a bath when you get your period? Wouldn't it be messy?

Generally the menstrual flow stops when you have a bath and then starts again very soon afterward. So, it's absolutely okay to have a bath or shower, and no, it probably won't be messy. The flow usually also stops when you go swimming, but it's probably a good idea to use a tampon then.

• ▲ •

*When my girl-friend has her period, she gets moody
and cries easily, or picks a fight for no reason at all.*

Some females experience mood swings just before or
during menstruation, because of the changes in their
hormone levels and the excess fluid in their tissues. It
might help if she reduced her salt intake at this time, ate
foods rich in vitamins B and C, got lots of sleep, and
avoided stress and anxiety. Stimulants such as coffee,
tea, cocoa and cola beverages may aggravate the situation.

If her symptoms are severe, the condition is called
pre-menstrual syndrome (PMS), and she should see her
doctor.

•　▲　•

*Whenever I get my period I get such bad cramps I can't
even get out of bed.*

Some kids really do have severe menstrual cramps, and
these can really lay you low. If you are fearful of
cramps, and anticipate that they will be severe, then
they will probably be even worse. You tense up at the
first twinge, then groan and brace yourself for the next
one; this gets your muscles working against you, making the cramps feel even more painful.

This is not to say that cramps are all in your head.
They are not. The medical name for them is dysmenor-
rhea.

You may just have to flake out with a hot water
bottle until the cramps go away. But if you really do
have difficult periods, ask your family doctor for a
prescription for an anti-prostaglandin medication. You

take two pills as soon as you feel the cramps coming on. If you still have pain after an hour, take one more. They really work; kids call them "magic blue pills." They are non-narcotic and non-addictive.

2

I Think About It All the Time

Sexual Fantasies

- Do you think you spend too much time fantasizing or day-dreaming?
- Do you ever think you will lose contact with reality and get lost in fantasy-land?
- Do you think your fantasies are wilder than anybody else's, and are you scared this means you're a pervert?
- Do you incorporate stuff from skin magazines or romantic scenes from TV, movies or books into your fantasies?
- Do you have several favourite fantasies?
- Is the person in your fantasy somebody featureless, vague, and blurry—someone you don't know or recognize?

If you answered yes to any of these questions, welcome to the club. Of all the sexual activities known to men and women, the ones we indulge in the most—and talk about the least—are our sexual fantasies. Everybody has fantasies, but we seldom share them with others, convinced that ours are weirder or kinkier than anybody else's.

Some fantasies are triggered by curiosity, while others seem to reflect our secret vision of ideal sexual activity. Although our ideal may be exaggerated, fantasy does allow us to explore what might be new and exciting and different.

Fantasy is a normal and enjoyable part of life. As long as you are able to recognize the difference between fantasy and reality, and do not act out fantasies that could be harmful to you or to others, then relax— you're perfectly okay.

If you have repeated fantasies that involve "abnormal" or unacceptable sexual behaviour—and if you are concerned about it—do talk to your doctor who will refer you to a therapist. Once you analyse and understand these fantasies, you can take control and feel good about yourself again.

•　▲　•

I am fifteen and I fantasize a lot. I pretend that I have a boy-friend, that he walks to school with me, and even though I've never "done it," I pretend that we sleep together. (I pretend my pillow is him.) Is this normal?

Fantasy is perfectly normal. We fantasize about everything—old boy-friend, new girl-friend, getting your own wheels, finishing school forever, earning lots of money, living on your own, winning the Nobel Prize. The list goes on. We fantasize through boring classes or a sinkful of greasy dishes. Sometimes we fantasize just because it's fun.

When our day-dreams involve sex we may be embarrassed, even ashamed. This is unfortunate, because romantic or sexual fantasies are beneficial: they help us develop a "love map," which defines the kind of partner, the kind of relationship we want for ourselves— and enables us to recognize them when they come along.

This is exactly what you are doing when you fantasize that you and your "lover" are enjoying all the nice, warm, loving things that you would like in a relationship. So when he does come along, you will know what you want and need, and can incorporate your fantasy into the "real thing."

You may be in love and very happy, but still find yourself occasionally fantasizing about some other person. This is fine and normal too. You are not being unfaithful; it just means you are human.

•   ▲   •

I dream about sex a lot. These dreams are really exciting. I have to admit I enjoy them. But I don't just dream about movie stars—sometimes it's guys I know: friends, my teachers, neighbours, even relatives. This really bothers me, because I have to face these people the next day! It's embarrassing.

I am impressed with your collection of gorgeous guys! Fantasizing is free, it isn't fattening, and as long as we don't try to make all our fantasies come true, they are harmless. Night-dreams, as compared to day-dreams, are really enjoyable; they happen all by themselves, without any help from us. But some people are upset by their sexual dreams because, unlike day-time fantasies, they are unable to control them.

The important thing is to recognize the difference between fantasy and reality. Your imagination can't hurt you—or anyone else—unless you make the mistake of trying to live out your dreams. You're right— it's embarrassing to face these guys the next day. But they need never know. So relax and enjoy.

•   ▲   •

I have a sexual fantasy that concerns me. Sometimes I like to fantasize that a man forces me to have sex with him. Does this mean I want to be raped?

Absolutely not. Rape is now called sexual assault, and no female has the idea that being beaten and dragged into the bushes or knocked to the cement in the underground parking lot is a fantastic way to have sex.

Fantasizing about something does not mean that you really want it. Sometimes it's hard to give yourself permission to have sex so instead you fantasize that it's being forced on you.

Your fantasy is a way for you to explore and experiment with your sexual feelings. The kind of fantasy you describe is very common, so don't worry. You do not want to be raped and no one should *ever* think that this is something *any* woman wants.

• ▲ •

The only way I can ejaculate while having sex with my girl-friend is to think about another girl while we are doing it. I like my girl-friend a lot and feel guilty about this. She'd be really upset if she knew about my fantasy.

This is not unusual, nor is it unhealthy. Perhaps you have the idea that "nice girls" don't have sex, and since your girl-friend is a nice girl, you may feel you shouldn't be doing these things with her. Fantasizing about another female, one you don't necessarily love and respect, may make sex okay and acceptable in your mind, allowing you to enjoy it.

Please know that nice girls do have sex and do enjoy it.

And yes, your girl-friend could well be upset if she knew of your fantasy. It's not necessary to tell her all—some things are best left unsaid.

• ▲ •

I am an eighteen-year-old girl. Sometimes I fantasize about having sex with another girl. I have a wonderful boy-friend, but I don't want to tell him and have him think I'm a lesbian. I have never had a homosexual experience, but I have to admit I have thought of trying it.

Nearly everyone has same-sex fantasies some time or other. This does not mean you are a homosexual or a lesbian. Nor does sexual experimentation with a person of the same sex. Although you and your boy-friend appear to have good communication, I understand your reluctance to share this fantasy with him. If you think he would feel threatened or turned off, then it's probably wise to keep it to yourself.

Researchers say that we may develop a particular sexual fantasy in early childhood and flip into this comfortable old scenario every once in a while. Sometimes we change and adapt our fantasies according to our needs at that particular time in our lives. This fantasy evidently meets your needs right now. But if it disturbs you, or if you find that same-sex fantasies are beginning to predominate, you might consider seeking some counselling.

Masturbation

Masturbation is defined as "touching the genitals for sexual arousal and satisfaction." It may be practised by yourself or with a partner. Slang expressions include "jerking off," "whacking off," and "playing with yourself."

Our attitudes toward masturbation have come a long way. Until recently, people were convinced that "self-abuse" (solitary masturbation) caused mental breakdown, blindness, or acne, and could result in congenital abnormality in future offspring. Early this century, parents instructed children to keep their hands above the covers when sleeping, or even tied their hands down at night. For kids who persisted in this "deviant" behaviour, there were rings with spikes that could be clamped around the penis at night to discourage nocturnal erections or touching the penis. A form of chastity belt prevented females from touching their genitals.

Many of our current myths are spin-offs of these misconceptions. So while kids laugh and say, "Masturbation is the occupation of the nation," many still have niggling doubts about possible side effects.

Hopefully, the following questions and answers will reassure you that masturbation is harmless, pleasurable and even beneficial.

• ▲ •

I baby-sit this little girl, aged eighteen months. When I change her diaper or put her in the tub I notice she likes

*to touch her genitals. When I put her to bed, she gets on
all fours and rocks. Is this normal?*

Absolutely. Like most kids, this little girl has discovered that it feels good to touch her genitals, so she does
it every chance she gets. It's not very different from a
child's discovery of the pleasures of thumb-sucking,
and it's just as harmless. Certainly it calls for no intervention on your part.

Parents sometimes make a big deal out of masturbation and succeed only in making the child feel it is dirty,
shameful or harmful. A more constructive approach, as
children get older, is to tell them gently that masturbation is a private matter, to be done in your own room,
not at the dining-room table or on the subway! That
way kids are spared humiliation and guilt, and simply
made aware that there is an appropriate time and place
for this activity.

• ▲ •

*Do girls masturbate? How do they do it? Does it feel as
good for them as it does for guys?*

Females certainly can and do masturbate. They enjoy it
every bit as much as males do, and can be very innovative about their masturbatory practices. Some touch
their genitals with their fingers. Others squeeze a pillow
between their legs, or simply squeeze their legs together.
Some straddle the arm of a chair or the side of a
bathtub, and simply rock. Others use a spray of water
from the shower head—"Don't just turn on the shower;
let the shower turn you on!" Some prefer a dildo or
vibrator (penis-shaped sex toys) for stimulation. Some

become sexually aroused while bicycling or horseback riding. One fifteen-year-old told me she accidentally discovered she could reach "a fantastic high" by sitting cross-legged on the floor, watching TV and rubbing her heel against her genitals.

Most females fantasize while they are masturbating. Some imagine that they are making love with someone famous and unattainable—a pop singer or movie star. Others like to pretend that they are with their own boyfriends, and they play back a mental video—a favourite memory or romantic fantasy. Females, like males, frequently masturbate just before going to sleep.

Occasionally, young women masturbate but do not identify and label the activity as such because they regard it as unacceptable.

Most females have masturbated by the time they reach their twenties. As well, most experience their first orgasm with masturbation, either solitary or with a partner—"mutual masturbation" or "heavy petting." By experimenting with masturbation, a female soon learns what pleases her. This helps her to become familiar with her own body, comfortable with her sexuality, and also teachers her what triggers orgasm for her—information she can relay to her partner. In fact, if an adult female is unable to reach orgasm, a therapist would urge her to masturbate. So there—it's actually therapeutic!

•   ▲   •

Can I hurt myself by touching the clitoris? Will I lose my virginity, get an infection, or hurt my vagina by masturbating?

It's very unlikely that you could damage yourself by touching the clitoris—it's so sensitive that, if you get a bit too enthusiastic, it won't feel good and you'll simply stop. You can't give yourself an infection by touching the clitoris, either. And don't worry about getting totally hooked on self-stimulation—that's just a myth.

And no, you do not lose your virginity by masturbating. A virgin is someone who has never had sexual intercourse. So you can do "everything but" and still technically be a virgin.

Nor will you hurt your vagina. It's lined with heavy-duty mucous membrane that is very elastic and resistant to injury. So it's okay—not to worry.

•　▲　•

Is it true that masturbation helps menstrual cramps?

Yes, it is true. Many females find that if they masturbate and experience orgasm, they become completely relaxed and the cramps seem to go away.

If it works for you—great. If you still have severe cramps—see your doctor.

•　▲　•

How do males masturbate?

A male usually holds the shaft of his penis with one hand or both. Using saliva or petroleum jelly as lubrication, he rhythmically slides his hand up and down, while fantasizing and becoming sexually aroused until he ejaculates. Most males also experience orgasm when this happens.

As infants, boys (like girls) often play with themselves simply because it feels good. At puberty, a male may begin to masturbate more frequently, sometimes several times a day, fantasizing while gazing at pictures in skin magazines for inspiration. Masturbation may become less frequent once a male becomes sexually active, but it rarely ceases entirely. Most men masturbate, even after marriage, and many married couples incorporate mutual masturbation into their lovemaking.

Occasionally, boys masturbate together. Some touch, stroke or rub each other's genitals to the point of ejaculation. I've even heard of jerk-off sessions where guys stand in a row and masturbate to see who will last longest or shoot the farthest. These same-sex experiences are a normal and natural part of growing up, and are not an indication of homosexuality, nor will they lead to homosexuality.

Masturbation is perfectly normal and natural for both males and females.

· ▲ ·

Doesn't masturbation make your acne worse?

Absolutely not. Here are some other things it will *not* do:

- It will not make hair grow on the palms of your hands.
- It will not make you go blind, deaf or bald.
- You will not wear out your penis/clitoris.
- It will not make your penis curve or fall off, nor will it leave finger indentations on your penis.

- It will not drive you crazy or turn your brain to mush.
- It will not make you a homosexual or lesbian.
- You will not become addicted to it.

Some religions and cultures forbid masturbation. If someone from such a background tried masturbation, then felt guilty about it, he or she might not enjoy the experience and may feel reluctant to repeat it. If this is your decision, that's fine. While it's normal to masturbate, it's also normal not to.

It's up to you—you call the shots!

• ▲ •

Is it normal to masturbate three times a day, seven days a week? Can you use up your sperm so you won't be able to have kids when you're older?

It is absolutely normal, and you will be okay—though you may not have much time left for anything else! Your body is constantly manufacturing sperm; it's not as though you start with a fixed supply that you have to ration throughout your life-time. Sperm have a fourteen-day life-span during which they form, ripen, mature, age, disintegrate, and then are absorbed back into the system. So you can't use them up—fortunately.

I wouldn't be concerned unless masturbation were to become your overriding preoccupation, to the point where you spend all your time locked in your room masturbating and have no interest in being with your friends and family, doing your homework, watching TV, playing hockey, meeting girls. . . . Anyone who withdraws in this way for the sole purpose of masturbating probably has big problems with self-confidence and self-esteem and would benefit from counselling. Otherwise—you're fine.

• ▲ •

My mother caught me masturbating, and I am so embarrassed now.

Most parents expect their sons to experiment with masturbation, and are willing to accept that boys will be boys. Daughters, on the other hand, often get a lecture: "You could hurt yourself"; "You might get an infection"; "Nice girls don't do that. . . ."

Even though some parents know that masturbation is normal, they are embarrassed to talk about it with their kids, and they have difficulty accepting the fact that *their* "babies" are growing up and have sexual feelings. If your mother feels this way, it might be better to wait till you and she are more comfortable with the topic before discussing it.

• ▲ •

Do married people still masturbate?

Absolutely! There is no reason either partner should stop masturbating just because they are married. Even if they have regular, satisfying sexual relations, they may wish to masturbate for any number of reasons. Sometimes one partner is interested in having sex and the other isn't. One partner may be absent or ill. Or, there may be times when the relationship is strained and the emotional intimacy just isn't there. Masturbation can satisfy the urge until they find themselves on the same wavelength again.

Many married couples masturbate as part of their sexual activity together. Masturbation doesn't necessarily compete with intercourse; rather, the two complement each other. So don't think once you're married you'll never masturbate again. You can go on masturbating as long as you find it pleasurable.

• ▲ •

I just don't want to masturbate! I can't imagine doing it.

Obviously you have strong negative feelings about masturbation at this time. I admire your self-awareness and am glad you know what is right for you.

Your feelings about masturbation may change in the future. I hope you continue to check out your feelings and allow changes to occur. Attitudes and values that are constantly re-evaluated permit personal growth and development. And if your feelings don't change—that's okay too. Don't feel that you are different or that there is anything wrong with you. You're fine—just as you are. Masturbation is not everybody's cup of tea!

3

What's Love Got to Do With It?

In a word—everything. But teenagers are always falling madly into or out of the roller coaster ride that is love. What is the difference between love and infatuation? Probably the biggest difference is time. Love lasts; infatuation doesn't.

We know many kinds of love—family, friends, God, pets. But this is different. The desire for intimacy, understanding, acceptance, approval, and appreciation, combined with the devotion, commitment, caring and concern that you feel for your beloved, are all essential for love.

You can love more than once; you can love different people for different reasons. Given enough time, you can grow to love anybody. What started out as a wonderful friendship could evolve into a long-term, loving relationship. Or you may meet someone once, and POW —you are in love. It could just be chemistry, or it could be the real thing.

But being in love does not mean you have to have sex. If you're in love, sex can wait till you are both certain and ready.

Why do girls find it easier to be intimate than guys?

There isn't a clear answer to this one. Feelings don't translate into data. But researchers agree that most females seem to have a greater number of intimate friends than males do.

Most of us tend to conform to society's expectations of "appropriate behaviour" for males and "appropriate behaviour" for females. Because males are expected to be aggressive, competitive and in control of their feelings at all times, they are less likely than females to risk self-disclosure, which is necessary for intimacy. Even when males would like to be intimate, they may find themselves trapped by expectations of "male behaviour." So, males are more likely to share only their achievements and accomplishments with their friends, while females will share their feelings, failures, hopes and dreams. Males sometimes feel it is safer to confide in females rather than other males—females seem less competitive and threatening, more understanding and accepting.

These may seem like generalizations, but you can see them at work in your own behaviour. Girl-friends spend hours on the phone together, sharing secrets, giggling, exploring their feelings and reactions. They are therefore better able to do the same with their boyfriends. Although attitudes are changing, young males still find it difficult to risk revealing their thoughts and feelings, even to their best friends. Sad—because we learn about intimacy first from our same-sex friendships.

• ▲ •

How do you let someone know you like him?

Easy—anything from dropping your books outside his locker to asking him to meet you in the library to do a project together. "Accidentally" bump into him after school or phone him with a history question. Or you can tell your best friend you'd like to meet him. He may hear about it and if he's interested he'll let you know.

Sometimes it's easier to go out with a gang the first time rather than with him alone. Tell him you're going to a movie, a hockey game or a concert with a few friends and ask him if he'd like to join you. It's perfectly okay for a girl to ask a guy out. You do not have to wait for him to call. Besides, he'd probably be very pleased to find out that you like him.

All these work—believe me!

•   ▲   •

How do I know if I am in love?

If you think you are in love, you are in love. It may not be the "hand in hand . . . walk into the sunset together . . . forever and ever" kind of love, but that wonderful glow, that total acceptance, that intense intimacy— that, for you, is love, at least right now. It's glorious, but it may not last forever, so enjoy it while it's there.

There are a few things you need to know about love. Love changes. It's never static; it evolves. It generally starts out as mad, passionate, flaming love. After about six months, the feeling mellows into what is called compassionate love. This is a quieter state, more comfortable, more predictable, less intense. You're not falling out of love, but it is changing. The relationship becomes deeper, warmer, and there is familiarity and comfort. The level of trust is high, and communication is open and honest. Wow—that's *love*.

Then reality sets in. You notice that he sometimes forgets to call when he said he would. Or maybe he is not a very good driver. He, on the other hand, finds that you schlep around in sweats and running shoes more than he would like, and gets upset when you go to the movies with your girl-friends instead of watching TV with him. Now you dare to disagree with him; or he argues with you. This is scary. Should this be happening if it's love?

Of course it should, and it must. The dynamics of your relationship are changing. Rather than deny the differences and the conflicts, you learn to find ways of resolving them, or making compromises, so that the relationship is not threatened. Having realistic expectations of each other helps a lot.

At this point there is a natural drawing back, or retreat, from the intense intimacy of your early days together. While that time was special and wonderful, the intensity would be unbearable if it went on forever. You would smother each other. So the pulling-away process allows you to reclaim your individuality and make some elbow room for yourselves. You are both able to keep your own friends and interests outside your shared relationship.

In time you find that there is a natural ebb and flow to intimacy: it moves from peaks to valleys to peaks again. Periods of intense involvement with your partner may be followed by a drawing back. As long as you are able to share your feelings with your partner, the relationship will continue to develop.

Being in love is one of life's great joys. So savour

every moment. And even if this particular love doesn't last—that's okay. It was wonderful and it *will* happen again.

• ▲ •

I think I'm in love with my science teacher. It's getting harder and harder to concentrate in his class.

I don't think there is a female alive who has not been "madly in love" with a teacher or professor. You idolize him; you practically drool in his class. It feels much more intense than having a crush on Bono or Michael J. Fox.

If you are able to be objective and honest you will admit that this is simply a fantasy. Your teacher is doing *nothing* to encourage you but you are imagining long, in-depth meaningful conversations with him. The fantasy is safe and will help you recognize true love when it comes along. But it is not so great in terms of your final exam in science. You have to develop the ability to separate fantasy from reality—and the reality is that you have to get a credit in science. So every time you find yourself lost in a daydream you must snap out of it and concentrate on the class.

This is not a putdown, but next year you will have a new teacher and a whole new fantasy love life. It's one way of getting through school!

• ▲ •

Girls have the idea that all guys are interested in is sex. It doesn't matter to them if they love the girl or not. Do you think this is true?

Absolutely not! We often have the idea that males will do it with any available female but most males are very selective about their choice of a partner. They want to care about their partner and are just as unsure, nervous, and anxious about sex as females—perhaps even more so.

Now, I grant you there are some super studs who are "on the make" with everybody and anybody—but most guys, like girls, are looking for someone special.

• ▲ •

Do you have to have sex if you are "in love"?

No, you do not have to have sex just because you are in love. You only have sex because it is what you want when you want it and are ready. Sex does not prove love and commitment. There are so many other ways to express love: consideration, communication, affection, warmth and understanding.

Sexual activity is only one way of expressing "intimacy," and it has no meaning unless it is what you both *really* want to do.

• ▲ •

I have a boy-friend and I really love him, but I don't want to have sex. He is not pressuring me but I know he wants to do it.

Now—you're a winner—a lady who is not ready to have sex, knows it and wants to say "no."

So how do you say "no" without risking the relationship? Well—it is much easier if you can put it in terms of "I feel . . ."

- we are too young for sex
- scared
- uncomfortable and embarrassed just thinking about it
- virginity is important—I want to do it the first time with my husband
- my parents would be so upset and I couldn't cope with that
- I am just not ready for it yet!

Now—when you say "no" you have to be gentle but firm. If your boy-friend tries to convince you, you have to say, "No and I mean it."

It's nice that he finds you attractive, that he's turned on by you. But this doesn't mean you have to have sex. Sounds like you two have a great relationship. I doubt that your boy-friend would *want* to have sex if he knew you didn't.

• ▲ •

Why do some girls tease guys?

Guys call it teasing. Females call it flirting. The difference is females see flirting as a fun thing to do—a harmless sport; whereas males see it as manipulation and it makes them angry. Either way it is a way of establishing the power position. She teases, turns him on, gets him all hot and bothered, then she may laugh, put him down, play coy (who me?) and walk away leaving him feeling foolish and vulnerable. It's not a great game to play for the following reasons:

- She can get a reputation for being a "tease."
- Guys can get into playing the same game and both of you can end up being emotionally hurt.

- Males and females do not learn to relate to each other honestly without manipulation.
- It is only a temporary boost to her ego and it is actually damaging to her self-esteem in the long run.
- She runs the risk that some male may get hostile and sexually assault her.

So teasing is not a great idea and guys might find it beneficial to avoid females who "tease" this way.

• ▲ •

All my friends have a girl-friend. I'm so lonely. I want somebody.

I must confess, this is the one question I have the most trouble with. Everybody is preoccupied with the task of finding "the perfect someone" to make their life complete. Generally, we have totally unrealistic expectations of what a partner will do for our dull, boring and lonely life. So we pin our hopes on some fantasy partner who will rescue us; make us feel complete.

What you need to do is to develop your own interests, hobbies, sports and pastimes so you are not dependent on somebody else to make you feel good. And this way, when you do meet someone you will have a great deal to contribute to a relationship rather that relying on her to make your life complete.

Being involved in a lot of different activities also exposes you to a lot more people—on the ski tow, at night school, with a church youth group—thus increasing the probability you will meet a person who likes doing the same things as you.

But don't start to feel desperate, because when you are desperate your antennae are up and you are almost frantic in your search. This neediness is picked up by others and scares them off. They fear that they can't possibly meet your needs, so they are not willing to even try.

So if you are lonely pursue your own interests. Feel okay all by yourself. Once this happens somebody will come along to join you and make it more enjoyable.

Sorry about that. I know it's not what you wanted to hear. You wanted a magic quickie answer, but *you* are the magic quickie answer.

•   ▲   •

My boy-friend and I can talk about anything, but when it comes to sex, forget it. I enjoy sex with him but if I don't want to do it, he says I don't love him. How can I say no?

Having sex does not prove you love him. I am concerned that he is trying to manipulate you into feeling guilty about refusing or rejecting him.

Tell him how you feel. Here are a few hints on improving your communication with him:

- *Choose the right time and place.* It's not a good idea to discuss touchy subjects when both of you are angry. Agree to wait till things have cooled down and you're both ready to listen to each other.

- *Avoid blaming him; use "I messages" instead.* Identify your own feelings—"When you do this . . . it makes me feel. . . ." Then he will see how his behaviour is affecting you.

- *Invite him to share his feelings.* When he responds, give him some feedback by re-phrasing what he's just said. Then he'll know that you're listening and have understood him correctly.

- *Stay on topic.* Don't let him rush you so that he can jump in with his own observations. If you're having trouble following his reasoning, say so, with something like: "Do you mean . . .?"

There are a few approaches you could try using to open the lines of communication with your boy-friend:

—"I don't want to have sex unless it's what we both want. It feels better then."
—"I don't like having to justify why I don't want to have sex. Just because you want to have sex doesn't mean I have to."
—"How would you feel about being pressured into something you didn't want to do?"

Your boy-friend's response will tell you a lot about whether it's worth continuing the relationship.

Do not allow yourself to be pressured into having sex. You are not responsible for his sexual satisfaction; if he's feeling horny, he can always masturbate to re-lieve the pressure. Sex is for mutual pleasure and satis-faction. You have the right to do it when you are interested and the right to refuse it when you are not.

• ▲ •

I met a wonderful guy, but there are a few problems. He is thirty-five years old and I am eighteen. Also, he is married and has two children. He says he loves me, and I love him. Do you think I'm crazy?

Not legally, certifiably insane, but you are not blessed with an overabundance of the smarts just now. It's not hard to imagine why you might be attracted to each other. To him you are exciting, young and attractive—also inexperienced and impressionable. He may feel he can mould you to suit his fantasy. You, on the other hand, see him as older, wiser, more experienced, accomplished, warm, maybe sad and needy. But the odds of this relationship surviving are, to put it bluntly, lousy.

Apart from the fact that he's almost twice your age, let's consider that he is married. If he were to leave his wife, how would you feel knowing that you had broken up his marriage and caused so much unhappiness to her and their children? Could you cope with being part of a dirty divorce? How would you feel about a man who would walk away from his responsibilities as a husband and father just to be with you? Would you want to be a weekend mother to his kids? On the other hand, he may choose those responsibilities over his relationship with you, and refuse to leave his wife. Then you'd be left alone and hurting. You're in a no-win situation.

Have you asked yourself what he wants from you? Does he really want to divorce his wife and have a long-term relationship with you, or are you just somebody new, exciting and different?

The proof that you are not crazy lies in the fact that you had enough sense to write and ask my opinion—and babes, you got it. This relationship might work as a fantasy, but I think you're smart enough to realize that it must not be allowed to go any further than that.

In my view, anyone who is married is off-limits. Smart ladies are the ones who simply say, "I don't date married men."

•▲•▲•▲•▲•▲•▲•▲•▲•▲

4

AIDS and You:
Safer Sex

AIDS: You've heard a lot about it ...
... but how much do you really know?

AIDS has been in the headlines since the first cases were reported in 1981. For much of that time, it was a condition we didn't know much about.

Mostly we knew it was scary—and a good deal of media coverage made it seem even more frightening.

We know more about AIDS now. And we know that being scared isn't the best response.

Being *informed* is.

When you get the facts about AIDS, you can figure out how to deal with it in a safe and sensible way. This chapter will give you the basic facts about AIDS as we presently understand them. But research continues, and our information changes rapidly. So the best way to keep yourself informed about AIDS is through books, TV and newspapers, and discussions with your parents, teachers and friends.

The information in this chapter is based on two

pamphlets prepared by the AIDS Committee of Toronto, "AIDS: Get the Facts" and "This is a Test." If you would like copies of these pamphlets, write to the AIDS Committee of Toronto. The address is listed in the back of this book.

• ▲ •

What is AIDS?

AIDS—Acquired Immune Deficiency Syndrome—is a condition in which the body's defence system against illness is knocked out. This means that people with AIDS get diseases that most of us can easily fight off. It is these diseases, not AIDS itself, that can be fatal.

• ▲ •

What causes AIDS?

In 1983 a virus was discovered that we now know leads to AIDS. It is called HIV (human immunodeficiency virus). HIV is commonly referred to as the "AIDS virus" although that is not the proper medical or scientific term.

• ▲ •

Does the virus always have the same effect?

No. Like many viruses, HIV affects different people in different ways.

• HIV can live in the body for many years with no visible effects. Some people have HIV in their system, but don't show any symptoms of infection. Many of these people remain healthy, although they can infect others through blood, semen or vaginal secretions.

- Some people who have been infected with HIV show some symptoms of AIDS-related illness, but do not have a life-threatening disease. This is called ARC or Aids Related Complex.

- Some people's immunity against disease is so damaged by HIV that they develop very serious illnesses, such as Kaposi's sarcoma, a skin cancer, or PCP, a form of pneumonia. When a person has one of these diseases—which almost never occur in people with healthy immune systems—and when HIV infection is the only known cause of damage to the immune system, then that person is said to have AIDS.

Until recently, most people diagnosed with AIDS died within two years. However, as we learn more about how to help the body fight the virus, more people with AIDS have been able to live longer.

We do not know what long-term effects HIV infection may have on people who do not have AIDS. We can't predict how many people who are infected will stay healthy, nor which ones will develop AIDS. The possible "co-factors" that might help HIV cause AIDS are not known.

• ▲ •

How is the virus that causes AIDS spread?

In order for infection to start, a sufficient quantity of HIV has to get into the bloodstream. There are only a few very specific ways that that can happen—and a lot of ways that it can't.

You *cannot* pick up the virus that causes AIDS through casual, day-to-day social contacts.

You *cannot* get the virus from:
- telephones
- toilet seats
- swimming pools
- whirlpools
- hugging a person with AIDS
- sharing glasses or dishes
- buses and subways
- someone sneezing near you

Tens of thousands of health care workers have come in contact with people with AIDS. Only a few have become infected, and those few have done so by accidentally sticking themselves with contaminated needles, or because they did not follow proper infection control procedures.

No one has ever been infected with HIV simply by sharing a home with anyone who has AIDS, despite very close contacts over long periods of time.

So, how can the virus be spread?

- The most common way HIV (AIDS virus) is transmitted is through sexual activity in which the semen or blood of one person enters the bloodstream of another.

  This can happen in vaginal or anal intercourse without a condom, in oral sex on a man when there is ejaculation, in oral sex on a woman, and while sharing sex toys.
- Drug users who share needles or syringes risk being infected. Infected blood can be passed

from one person to another this way.
- Women who carry the virus may infect unborn children in pregnancy or during childbirth.
- People who received a blood donation between 1979 and November 1985 run a very small risk of having been infected. Since November 1985 the Red Cross has been screening all blood donations to find infected blood and make sure it is not used.

• ▲ •

Can I get AIDS from mosquitos?

No. HIV is not spread by insects.

• ▲ •

I've heard the AIDS virus is in saliva. Can I get AIDS from kissing?

Very small traces of the AIDS virus have been found in the saliva of infected people. However, of the over 50,000 cases of AIDS reported worldwide, not one has been caused by simple kissing. However, if there is any break in the mucous membrane or skin, then you are at risk.

• ▲ •

Can you get AIDS by giving blood?

You *cannot* get AIDS by donating blood. All needles used to take blood donations are used only once and then thrown away.

Before November 1985, some people were infected with HIV when they *received* blood transfusions. But since that time all donated blood has been tested for evidence of HIV infection. Being infected by a transfusion is now very unlikely.

• ▲ •

Who can get AIDS?

Viruses don't discriminate. *Anyone* can be affected by the virus that causes AIDS.

AIDS was once thought of as a "gay disease." In North America it was first discovered in homosexual men. But it was soon found in others as well—people who had received infected transfusions before blood donations were screened, users of needle-borne drugs, and children whose mothers carried HIV and passed it on during pregnancy or childbirth.

In Canada and the US, more than 30 percent of people with AIDS are *not* gay or bisexual men. In Central Africa, where AIDS is more common, it affects men and women in equal numbers.

With AIDS, it doesn't matter who you are—a man or a woman, Black or white, heterosexual or homosexual.

It matters what you *do*.

• ▲ •

Is there a cure or vaccine?

No, not yet.

Some drugs are now being used to slow down the

growth of the AIDS-causing virus in the body, or to
stave off serious infections. Others are being tested.
These drugs can relieve some symptoms, and help
people with AIDS or AIDS-related illnesses live longer.
But they are not a cure.

Testing of possible vaccines is going on, but it will be
a long time before we know if they work. Even if an
effective vaccine is found, it will be years before it is
widely available.

The only way we can stop AIDS right now is by
learning how to keep ourselves and others from being
infected with HIV, the virus that causes AIDS.

•   ▲   •

Can you tell if someone has the AIDS virus?

You can't. Many people have the virus but look and
feel perfectly healthy. They may not even know themselves that they have the virus. *But they can still pass
the virus on to others.* That's why it is so important to
always practice safer sex.

•   ▲   •

What is safer sex?

Safer sex means protecting yourself and your partner
from HIV. We know for sure that the virus can be
transmitted through blood and semen. Sexual activity
is one of the most likely ways for semen and blood
from one person to get into the bloodstream of another
person. Tiny breaks in the lining of the mouth, vagina
and rectum are common. You don't usually notice

them—but the virus can get through them so it's important to follow these guidelines when you're involved in a sexual relationship:

HIGH RISK SEX
- Any act that gets blood or semen into the mouth, rectum, or vagina is high-risk and must be avoided. These include:
- Vaginal or anal intercourse without a condom
- Oral sex on a man
- Oral sex on a woman
- Sharing sex toys (i.e. vibrators)

LOWER RISK SEX
Some sexual acts present only a small risk of infection:
- Oral sex on a man with a condom
- Vaginal sex with a condom and foam
- Deep kissing, except when there are open sores or cuts in the mouth

SAFE SEX
Many sexual practices cannot transmit HIV and are perfectly safe:
- Hugging
- Light kissing
- Licking skin or nipples
- Massage
- Masturbation with your partner

And don't forget, there's always NO SEX. Until you're involved in a long term, committed relationship you may not wish to be involved in sex at all.

•　▲　•

How do condoms help to protect you from the AIDS virus?

A condom is a thin sheath that fits over the entire erect penis. When a male ejaculates, the semen is collected in the condom and does not come in contact with his partner. Since HIV is found in semen, the condom prevents the spread of the virus. Small amounts of the virus can be present in vaginal secretions so if a male is wearing a condom he is protected from getting the virus. Condoms also protect you from some other sexually transmitted diseases and, when used with contraceptive foam, are an effective method of birth control.

•   ▲   •

Where can you buy condoms?

- Condoms can be bought at all drug stores. In most stores they will be on the open shelves in the section where birth control products are sold. You will not have to ask anyone for a package.
- Make sure you buy *latex* condoms with a reservoir (nipple) end. Do not buy condoms made of any other material. Only latex prevents leakage.
- Buy condoms lubricated with spermicide containing nonoxynol-9, which has been shown to kill HIV. The lubricant on some condoms does not contain nonoxynol-9 so be sure to check the labelling on the package. (Some females may find that nonoxynol-9 will irritate their vagina. If this is the case, your partner should use a

condom which is not lubricated with spermicide containing nonoxynol-9. Spermicide can also cause irritation of the rectum, so although you must use condoms if you have anal sex, they must be lubricated but not with spermicide.)

- Buy new condoms every few months. Condoms get old and are more likely to break so if the expiration date on your package has passed, throw it out even if you haven't used all the condoms and buy a new pack.

- Don't be shy about buying condoms. Using condoms is regarded as responsible behaviour, so please don't be embarrassed about it.

• ▲ •

Do condoms come in more than one size?

Nope, one size only. So you don't have to do any measuring before you go to the store.

• ▲ •

Is it okay for girls to buy condoms?

Yes, it is absolutely okay. In fact, forty percent of condoms are sold to females and many condom companies are gearing their advertising toward them. Having safer sex means using condoms and the responsibility should be shared equally by males and females.

• ▲ •

HOW DO YOU USE A CONDOM?

Using condoms means just that—*using them*. It means buying them, having them with you when you have sex, taking them out and putting them on before the penis gets anywhere near the vagina.

It's a good idea for both males and females who haven't used condoms before to buy a package, take it home and unwrap a condom to see what it looks like. Males who aren't accustomed to using condoms should practise putting one on alone before using them with a partner. Here's how you do it:

- Remove the rolled condom from the package.
- Put the condom on the penis as soon as it is hard, *before* you start to have sex or foreplay. Don't put the condom on only when you are ready to enter your partner—it may be too late. Drops of semen can ooze from the uncovered penis before ejaculation, and may infect or make your partner pregnant.
- Do not unroll the condom before you put it on. Instead, hold the condom at the head of the penis, squeeze the air out of the tip to leave room for the semen, and then gently unroll it onto the penis down to the base, making sure there are no air bubbles. This is important because it helps to prevent the condom from breaking.
- Even if you are using a condom lubricated with spermicide, you might find it difficult to enter your partner. So if you need more lubrication, use a lubricant that is water soluble—like K-Y, or Lubafax. Never use an oil-based lubricant like petroleum jelly or baby oil on a condom. They can weaken latex and make the condom break.

- Condoms should not break if used properly but it can happen. This is why females should always use foam as a back-up method whenever you have sex (see page 102). Contraceptive foam also contains nonoxynol-9 and provides protection against HIV and pregnancy. But foam shouldn't be used alone. It has to be used with a condom.

TO REMOVE THE CONDOM:

- Withdraw the penis from your partner soon after you ejaculate. Do not wait until the penis gets soft. If you do, the ejaculate can spill out of the condom and infect your partner or make her pregnant. Keep the used condom away from your partner's body, especially the genitals.
- Hold on to the condom at the base of the penis while you are pulling out to make sure it doesn't leak or slip off.
- Remove the condom and flush it down the toilet.
- Rinse off your hands and penis.

SOME DON'TS:

- Don't ever use a condom more than once.
- Don't store condoms in the glove compartment of a car. They can be damaged by heat.
- Don't carry condoms in your hip pocket or wallet for a long period of time. Your body heat can weaken the latex.
- Don't twist, bite or damage the condom with your fingernails. Latex condoms are strong but even a tiny hole can allow ejaculate to leak out.

• ▲ •

What should I do if my partner doesn't want to use a condom?

You should say quite simply, "No condom, no sex," but here a few other approaches to take:

If your partner says:	You can say:
We're using the pill. We don't need a condom.	The pill doesn't protect us from AIDS or other sexually transmitted diseases. Only a condom does.
Condoms are no fun.	Neither is getting AIDS.
I haven't had sex in months. I know I don't have anything.	Either of us could have an infection and not know it. Let's not take any chances.
I don't have any condoms.	OK, let's just watch TV tonight and buy some tomorrow. We can fool around then.
We'll use one next time.	It only takes one time to get infected so we have to use condoms *every* time.
I love you! I wouldn't give you an infection!	I know you don't want to give me an infection and I don't want to give you one either. That's why we're going to use a condom.

I've never done it before so I couldn't have anything.	Well, I have and I want to protect you.
It destroys the spontaneity.	This way we can slow things down a bit and make it last even longer.

But if none of these works and your partner still refuses to use a condom, don't have intercourse. It's as simple as that.

• ▲ •

Is a rubber the same thing as a condom?

Yes. Rubber, sheik, and safe are all slang terms for condom.

• ▲ •

When I had sex for the first time with my girl-friend she had condoms ready to use. Does this mean she sleeps with a lot of guys?

No, not at all. It does not mean that your girl-friend "sleeps around." It *does* mean that she was attracted to you and hoped something would develop. She thought about it and was protecting both of you from HIV and other sexually transmitted diseases. She is thoughtful, aware and smart, all qualities to be admired. You're a lucky guy.

• ▲ •

Can you get AIDS from sharing a joint?

No. You will not get the virus from passing around a marijuana joint. HIV is spread by sharing needles and syringes used to inject drugs into the bloodstream. If you are an intravenous drug user *never* share needles and syringes. The best thing you can do is to get help for your drug problem. A local youth clinic or your doctor in your area can refer you to a drug treatment centre. And *always* practise safer sex.

• ▲ •

My boyfriend and I have been together for a year. Do we still have to practise safer sex?

People in relationships should remember that HIV can live in the body for many years without anyone knowing it's there. Even if you have only one partner now, you or your boyfriend may have picked up the virus before you met. If either of you were sexually active before you met or used needle-borne drugs, you should be having safer sex with each other.

• ▲ •

Can you take a test to find out if you have been infected with HIV?

Yes. The test was originally designed to screen blood donations, to keep infected blood out of the public supply used for transfusions. Your local health department will have information about where you can go for the test.

• ▲ •

How accurate is the test?

The test detects the presence of antibodies—substances produced by the body in response to infection by specific viruses. If the antibody to HIV is found—that is, if you test positive—it means HIV has entered your bloodstream at some point in your life. If you have not been infected by HIV, the test should show a negative result.

The test tells only whether the antibody is present. It does not detect the presence of HIV itself.

We do know, in the case of this virus, that having antibodies does not make you immune to AIDS.

In a very small percentage of cases, the test will give a false reading. Anyone who tests positive is tested again for confirmation. In rare cases, people will get a negative test result even when they have been infected. Some people do not produce antibodies to the AIDS virus but they can still infect others. That is why you must always practice safer sex.

• ▲ •

What does a positive test result mean?

If you test positive, it means that antibodies to the AIDS virus have been found in your blood. Remember—a positive test result tells you only that you have been infected by the AIDS virus at some point.

- It does not mean that you have AIDS or an AIDS-related illness.

- It does mean you should practice safer sex. It's important for other people because you may be able to pass on the virus.

But you should assume this is possible and take steps to prevent exposing others. If you get involved in a sexual relationship you have an obligation to inform your partner that you are carrying the virus. Your partner can then decide if he or she is willing to take the risk. You absolutely *must* practise safer sex, do not donate blood and if you are a drug user, do not share needles or syringes.

• ▲ •

What does a negative test result mean?

Testing negative means that no antibodies to HIV (AIDS virus) have been found in your blood. However, this does not mean you're home free. Because:

- It does not mean for sure that you haven't been infected by HIV (AIDS virus). You may have been exposed recently enough that your body hasn't yet had time to produce antibodies. We don't fully know how long this takes, but most people develop antibodies within three months. In some cases, however, antibodies never develop.

- It does mean you should continue to practice safer sex.

A negative test result does not protect you from AIDS infection.

You should still take precautions to prevent infecting others, and to avoid being infected in the future if you are not now.

● ▲ ●

A kid in my class has got AIDS from a blood transfusion. Any possibility I could get it?

None—unless you are sexually involved with that person or sharing needles.

This classmate can safely be included in all your activities, both athletic and social—and needs your friendship, support and understanding at this time.

You have a wonderful opportunity to show real leadership by reassuring the other kids, and by not allowing them to ridicule, isolate or put down this schoolmate.

Your acceptance, appreciation and approval will make life much easier for this person.

Your concern is understandable, and I am glad you inquired about your fears. Now you can do a lot to reassure others. Thank you!

5

Sue, I Think I've Got Something: STDS

For years, parents used the threat of venereal disease (VD) to deter teens from having sex. Today we speak of sexually transmitted diseases, or STDs for short.

With the recent addition of HIV (AIDS virus) to our list of STDs, it's more important than *ever* before that anyone who decides to be sexually active must practise "safer sex" (see chapter 4). Safer sex *is* smarter sex.

Sexually transmitted diseases are just that—you get them from sexual contact. You do not get them from doorknobs, toilet seats or drinking fountains. They are spread by intimate physical contact with another person, not necessarily intercourse. Using condoms is important, but they do not always protect you from *all* STDs.

While most STDs—other than HIV (AIDS virus)—are easy to treat, having one can be scary. Talking about STDs is what I call gross-out time. It's almost enough to put you off sex entirely. While I don't want to scare you, it is important to know about STDs, how to protect yourself from them and what to do if you think you've got one.

What do you do if you think you've caught a sexually transmitted disease?

Get yourself to a doctor or STD clinic immediately. A sexually transmitted disease will not clear up by itself, and can only get worse if left untreated. Do *not* try to treat it yourself. Leftover prescriptions of any kind will not help you. Do *not* have sex until you have been diagnosed and treated by a doctor, and told that you're okay.

If you don't want to go to your family doctor, look in the blue pages of the phone book under "Municipalities —Health Department." You can phone for the location and hours of an STD clinic near you. Some cities have "Sexually Transmitted Disease Hotlines." The number can be found in the white pages of the phone book. Or, you can check the Directory at the back of this book. Visits to government clinics are free, and so are most drugs that are prescribed, but you'd have to pay for medication prescribed by your family doctor.

The doctor or nurse will take your general medical history and run some tests specifically for STDs. A swab is taken of the infected area (i.e. the cervix, urethra, rectum, throat), and sent to the lab. A blood test may also be taken. You will be asked about *all* recent sexual contacts, and it's important that you answer honestly. You will not be lectured, put down or hassled.

So please, don't be embarrassed or ashamed about asking for help if you suspect you have an STD. These are diseases, just like a cold or flu. Getting proper treatment will make you feel better, will prevent serious complications and will keep you from spreading the disease to somebody else.

• ▲ •

I heard that if you have an STD and go to the doctor or clinic, they want your partner's name and address. Is this true?

Not usually. But if you have gonorrhea or syphilis, which are "reportable" diseases, everyone you've had sex with in the past two months will need to be notified and advised to get a check-up immediately. They may have the disease, not know it, and spread it to other sexual partners. Chlamydia may soon also be a reportable disease.

An STD nurse will contact your partner or partners. This is done very carefully and discreetly. It is confidential: names are *never* released. Your name will never be mentioned. A clinic nurse will simply tell them: "You have come in contact with a sexually transmitted disease. Please come to the clinic within the next few days." This call is followed up to ensure that all possible contacts are checked out and treated if necessary.

• ▲ •

Can you tell if someone has a disease just by looking?

What have you got in mind? Imagine it: there you are, in the heat of passion, and all of a sudden you whip out your flashlight and do a genital inspection. Would you know what you were looking for even if you saw it? And don't forget—many STDs have *no* symptoms at all.

Unless you're a skilled diagnostician, there is no way you can tell, just by looking, whether your partner has an STD. You could ask, of course; but your partner might not know about the infection, or might not answer truthfully. You can never be sure. So *always* practice safer sex as described in Chapter 4.

In a "quickie" sexual encounter, STDs are the last thing on anyone's mind. Good reason to avoid casual sex—it's too risky. Sex is safer—and better!—in a stable, loving, caring, committed, long-term relationship, where you are open and honest with each other. Then you eliminate the stress and anxiety of the unknown.

• ▲ •

Do you develop any immunity to STDs?

There is no immunity to any sexually transmitted diseases. You can get them again and again and again. If you really work at it, you can have more than one STD at the same time: gonorrhea, chlamydia, herpes, crabs and warts get along quite well together.

And then there's HIV (AIDS virus). So you have a lot of reasons to be careful, not only by limiting your choice of sexual partners, but also by practising "safer sex." These diseases are not choosy—so you have to be.

• ▲ •

I heard you can get STDs from a bathtub.

Depends on what you are doing in the bathtub! No, you won't get any sexually transmitted diseases, even if you have a bath right after an infected person.

Now, if you have sex in the bathtub, and your partner has an STD, then yes, there is a good chance you could get an STD. But don't blame the tub.

• ▲ •

How do you know if you've got gonorrhea?

Gonorrhea, also called the clap, a dose, or the whites, is spread through sexual contact only. One in five males who have it will have no signs or symptoms; most females who have it have no symptoms, although there may be some yellow discharge from the vagina.

Two to ten days after intercourse with an infected partner, males may have severe pain when urinating, and they need to urinate more frequently. Often there is a thick, yellow discharge—pus—from the penis. But sometimes the symptoms are hardly noticeable or there are none at all.

You and your partner should get to a doctor or STD clinic immediately, even if only one of you has symptoms. If gonorrhea is detected, treatment—in the form of a large dose of penicillin, either pills or a liquid, taken all at once—begins immediately. People who are allergic to penicillin are given tetracycline. The tetracycline pills are *not* taken all at once.

Occasionally gonorrhea resists treatment by penicillin or tetracycline, in which case another antibiotic is prescribed. Under no circumstances should you attempt to treat yourself. This is a disease that should be treated only by a doctor. And *don't* share medication with your partner. You won't be given enough to kill the infection in both of you.

You must go back to the doctor or clinic in one to two weeks for retesting. In the meantime, *no* sex until further tests show you're cured.

The best prevention against gonorrhea is to use foam and a condom lubricated with spermicide whenever you have sex, and avoid casual sex. (See page 102 for instructions on how to use foam and page 68 on how to use a condom.)

• ▲ •

What happens if I have gonorrhea but don't get treated?

I'm glad you asked. If gonorrhea is left untreated, the symptoms (discharge, burning) will eventually go away, but the infection will continue to spread inside the body. In males the infection may travel through the reproductive system and may cause permanent sterility. In females, the infection spreads up to the Fallopian tubes, where it may cause Pelvic Inflammatory Disease (PID), which can result in permanent sterility.

So you can see how important it is, if you suspect you have gonorrhea, for you and your partner to get treatment—fast.

• ▲ •

My boy-friend and I had a humungous fight because he got gonorrhea and swears he has not had sex with anyone but me. Now he's accusing me of messing around, but I wasn't.

Well, somebody's been messing around. Sorry to be so blunt, but the chances of getting an STD any other way are extremely remote.

This is a rough situation for both of you. Accusations and blaming, denial and guilt can put a real strain on your relationship, and may even cause it to break up unless you are both able to work through your anger, resentment and feelings of distrust.

If your boy-friend recognizes that his behaviour is jeopardizing not only the relationship, but your health as well, then perhaps you can forgive and forget and resolve never to let it happen again. No matter what, *you* must be checked for gonorrhea, even if you have no symptoms.

• ▲ •

What is syphilis?

Syphilis is a sexually transmitted disease that, because it is easily treated with antibiotics, was considered "under control" until recently. But it has reappeared, and is serious if not diagnosed and treated.

If you have sex with an infected person, you will probably develop an open, oozing sore a few weeks later. This chancre, as it is called, will appear in the area where sexual contact has occured, (genitals, mouth, finger or breast). The discharge from the sore carries the bacteria.

The chancre will heal, and you may think you are okay. But the bacteria continue to spread throughout your body and after a few more weeks, or up to six months, you may feel nauseated, tired and headachy, with muscular aches and pains. This stage may also be characterized by an outbreak of sores in the mouth and genital area, and a non-itchy rash all over your body, but especially on the palms and soles of your feet.

When these symptoms pass, the disease enters the latent phase. There may be no signs or symptoms, but the bacteria are still in the bloodstream and can cause blindness or severe damage to the heart, liver, bones and brain if the infection is left untreated.

A pregnant female who has syphilis can infect her unborn baby, who may die or be born with severe congenital deformities.

Syphilis is diagnosed with a simple blood test. It can be left untreated but the best prevention is to use foam and condoms lubricated with spermicide whenever you have sex, and avoid casual sex.

Don't take chances. It's your body, your life, and only you can be responsible for it.

• ▲ •

Help! I have these little blisters on my genitals. They itch and burn, then go away after about a week. I'm scared—could it be herpes?

It's difficult for me to know for sure so go to your family doctor or an STD clinic for an accurate diagnosis. But it could be herpes. Herpes simplex is a virus. There are two types—herpes simplex I and II. Type I causes cold sores, generally around the mouth, and is not necessarily a sexually transmitted disease. But if a person has herpes simplex I on their mouth and performs oral-genital sex on a partner, the partner could develop genital herpes.

Type II, called genital herpes, causes similar sores or blisters on the genitals. It is spread by genital-to-genital contact or genital-to-oral contact; or if your partner has active herpes, touches his or her genitals, then touches your genitals, there is a possibility that you could get herpes.

With genital herpes, two to twenty days after contact

the genitals may become oddly sensitive and tingly. These are called the prodromal symptoms. Then tiny blisters appear—usually on the penis or scrotum in males, and on the inner or outer labia, the vagina, or cervix in females. Both sexes may get blisters around the rectum, or on the inner thighs. The blisters hurt— they itch and burn, fill with fluid, break and ooze fluid that is loaded with the active virus. Because the blisters may be present on areas of the genitals that can't be protected by a condom, sex during this time, even with a condom, can spread the disease to your partner. Besides the blisters, you may experience nausea, headache, and generally feeling lousy.

The blisters last about a week to ten days. Then they crust over, but remain infectious for about another week. Only when the area is fully healed and normal is it safe to resume sex. But you must watch for the return of the prodromal symptoms. When you have these symptoms, you can infect someone else, so—no sex.

Diagnosis of herpes can be confirmed only by a doctor and only during an active outbreak of blisters.

Unfortunately there is no cure for genital herpes. There are some things you can do to relieve some of the discomfort: warm baths with one tablespoon of baking soda in the water, an ice pack on the affected area, aspirin or acetaminophen to ease pain, loose cotton underwear. Avoid wearing tight jeans and pantihose.

There is a medication, called acyclovir which may help. Your doctor will give you a prescription for it. It is an ointment applied directly to the herpes blisters, and appears to work well for the first outbreak, less well after that. It also comes in pills which appear to control the number of outbreaks. You must avoid pregnancy while taking this medicine.

A lucky few never experience another outbreak. But for some people, stress will be the trigger: fight with your boyfriend, fail an exam, smash the car and you've got the whole mess all over again. Or you may have a recurrence if you get a sunburn, and you may find that some foods trigger an outbreak. Females may experience a recurrence with every menstrual period. Herpes is unpredictable, it's miserable, and I'm sorry it happened to you. If it's any consolation, usually the first outbreak is the worst, and the disease is not fatal or life threatening. As you get older, the outbreaks tend to be less frequent and less severe.

• ▲ •

Because I have herpes, does that mean I cannot have sex, get married, or have kids?

No, it does not mean any of the above. But you must inform your partner before you get involved in sex. Partners have a right to know, so that they can decide whether they are willing to risk contracting the disease.

You must watch for any prodromal symptoms and absolutely avoid sex until this outbreak runs its course.

The herpes virus does not affect a male's ability to make a baby, nor would it cause any birth defects. A female carrying the virus can get married, get pregnant, and carry the pregnancy to full term. Because the baby could be infected during delivery if the mother has an outbreak at that time, the doctor in all probability will perform a Caesarean, or C-Section. The mother and baby would both be fine.

If you are single and have herpes, the possibility of meeting a partner who can accept this condition may seem remote. It's tough even to talk about it. But you have to.

•   ▲   •

If my girl-friend has cold sores on her lips and we have oral sex, will I get herpes?

If your partner has cold sores and performs oral sex on you, yes, you can get herpes simplex I on your genitals.

If you have cold sores, wash your hands frequently. Don't touch the sores and then touch other parts of your body—or anybody else's!

And if you or your partner has a cold sore—no fooling around, not even kissing, until it's all better. You don't need oral herpes, and you sure don't need the genital kind.

•   ▲   •

I have some funny bumps on my penis. What are they, and how do I get rid of them?

Only a doctor can tell for sure, but it sounds like genital warts. They are caused by a virus, and spread by sexual contact with an infected person. They appear as small, flesh-coloured, raised bumps on the penis, sometimes on the scrotum, occasionally in or around the rectum. Females may get them on the labia, around the vaginal opening, in the vagina, on the cervix, in or around the rectum. Males will probably notice if they have warts, but a female may be unaware that she has them until she feels a strange bump while inserting a tampon, or her partner discovers them during foreplay. They normally appear any time from three weeks to three months after contact with an infected person.

Genital warts are painless, although they may itch or burn a bit. If not treated, they multiply and grow in clusters, which are harder to treat.

Recent research indicates that there is a higher incidence of cervical cancer in females who have had warts on the cervix. Therefore, they should have a Pap smear done every six months rather than once a year, for early detection of any abnormalities.

Do *not* try removing genital warts yourself—go to a doctor or an STD clinic. If there are only a few warts, the doctor will protect the surrounding area with petroleum jelly, and then dab a liquid on the wart. Painless. Leave this on for four hours (no longer, since it may burn the area) and wash the genitals with soap and water. You may have to return for repeat treatments twice weekly until all the warts are gone.

If there are lots of warts, or if they are high up in the vagina, on the cervix, or in the rectum, the doctor will refer you to a specialist who will treat them with liquid nitrogen. Zap—finished! (The warts, not you!)

Neither method will damage or scar your genitals— not to worry.

I hate to be a killjoy, but I suggest you refrain from sex until all the warts are gone. Condoms provide some protection, but no guarantees.

As with all STDs, both partners should be checked and treated at the same time.

•   ▲   •

Does the stuff that removes warts on your hands work on warts on your penis?

No way! Any treatment for warts that you can buy at a drugstore is *not* safe to use on genital warts. If you think you have genital warts, see a doctor. Also:

- Do not try to use any household cleaning products or other strong disinfectants. You may burn yourself, perhaps severely.
- Do not use a razor blade to whittle away genital warts. This will *not* eliminate the virus and, in fact, may spread it.

Warts are common and sometimes stubborn to treat. So you and your partner should go to your doctor, as soon as possible.

• ▲ •

I've suddenly developed this yucky discharge and it itches and burns, especially when I go to the bathroom. Have I got VD?

Sounds like a classic yeast infection, but only your doctor will know for sure. Most females get at least one yeast infection in their life-time. Such infections are caused by spores—*Monilia* (also called *Candida albicans*). They are not generally sexually transmitted, but can be spread to your male partner.

Females get a thick, white vaginal discharge that looks like cottage cheese or yoghurt. The genitals become red, itchy, and sore and swollen, and there may be some pain while urinating.

The doctor will take a smear of cervical secretions to

confirm that it is a yeast infection. Then you will get a prescription for vaginal suppositories (three or seven, depending on your doctor's preference) or a cream that is inserted into the vagina with a special applicator.

At bedtime, have a bath and insert one suppository (or one applicator full of cream) into the vagina as high up as it will go. Wear cotton underwear and place a panty liner or mini-pad in the crotch before you go to bed. The medication will kill the infection while you sleep.

Next morning have a shower, and then, because some medication may still be leaking out, wear a panty liner. The symptoms may have disappeared, but use *all* the suppositories or cream to be sure there are no spores left to flare up later.

Yeast is normally present in the vagina, but can overgrow for a variety of reasons. Because the birth-control pill changes the acid-alkaline (or PH) balance of the vagina, females who take the pill are more vulnerable to yeast infections. Taking antibiotics also increases the risk of getting a yeast infection, since antibiotics kill *all* bacteria, including the beneficial ones that help to keep yeast spores under control. Females who are diabetic tend to be more susceptible to yeast infections.

If you have frequent yeast infections, one remedy that helps prevent flare-ups is acidophilus tablets, which may be bought without a prescription at a health-food store. You simply insert one into the vagina after sexual activity or after your menstrual period. But self-medication is not a good idea unless you're absolutely positive the infection is yeast.

Other tips:

- Since an infected female can pass yeast infection on to a male partner, be sure he uses a condom lubricated with spermicide.

- Avoid skin-tight jeans, nylon panties and pantihose, all of which prevent air from circulating around the genitals, making the area a better medium for yeast spores to grow.
- Yeast spores live in your digestive tract and are excreted with feces. So please, when you have a bowel movement, you must remember to wipe from front to back.
- Reduce the amount of sugar in your diet.

• ▲ •

Can guys get yeast infections?

You betcha! The penis becomes red, sore and irritated in reaction to the infection. Most males have no symptoms at all but may carry the spores under the foreskin and can reinfect females during sex—another good reason to use condoms.

As with all STDs, both partners should be treated at the same time. Males are prescribed a cream, which they apply daily for about a week. During that time, no sexual intercourse—or use a condom lubricated with spermicide.

• ▲ •

I keep hearing you talk about a new disease, chlamydia. What is it?

It's not new, but up until recently it was very difficult to diagnose. Chlamydia is caused by bacteria that are transmitted during sex with an infected partner. Both males and females can get the disease.

Chlamydia really scares me. It can cause permanent sterility, and in most cases you don't even know you've got it. Most females have no symptoms at all, although there may be a vaginal discharge and/or a burning sensation during urination. A few weeks after infection, females may experience lower abdominal pain. Males may have a dull, heavy pain in the groin, with a discharge from the penis and a burning on urination. But in some cases there are absolutely no symptoms whatever.

Chlyamydia is a sneaky disease, and the damage is permanent. An undetected infection in a female can cause Pelvic Inflammatory Disease (PID), which may result in sterility or ectopic (tubal) pregnancy in the future. Untreated chlamydia also causes sterility in males.

The disease is easier to prevent than to detect. So—back to basics: foam and condoms lubricated with spermicide are your best and only protection. When you go for your annual physical exam insist that your doctor check for chlamydia even if you don't have symptoms.

Luckily, once it is diagnosed, chlamydia is easy to treat. Both partners are prescribed large doses of antibiotics, and it's important to take all the pills to make sure you get rid of the infection. This one is serious.

• ▲ •

What is trich?

Short for trichomoniasis—it is a sexually transmitted disease caused by the protozoan *Trichomonas vaginalis*. While both males and females can carry the organism and spread it during sexual intercourse, usually only the female develops symptoms: the genitals become red, sore, itchy and swollen, and urination may be painful (for males too). There is a thin, runny, frothy, greenish vaginal discharge that smells like dead fish. Symptoms take from four to twenty-eight days from the time of infection to appear.

Non-sexual transmission is also possible. Trich can survive for a short time on warm, moist objects such as towels.

Trich can be treated only by a doctor, who will prescribe six pills taken orally all at once, and absolutely do not drink any alcoholic beverages for forty-eight hours, or you'll feel barfy. Both partners *must* be treated, or you'll continue to reinfect each other (the "ping-pong effect").

•   ▲   •

I heard you can get crabs from a toilet seat. Tell me this isn't true!

It is true. Crabs are pubic lice, about the size of the head of a pin. Because they are mobile, they can crawl onto the seat of a public toilet. You sit on the seat, and —you got them! Then they set up housekeeping in the pubic hair. They look like pepper sprinkled on the pubic area. The female crab lays her eggs (nits) on the pubic hair. These eggs appear as little white bumps, which won't pull off. The nits hatch, then the crabs crawl down to the skin and bite. Their saliva irritates the skin and it starts to itch—like mad.

Crabs are spread mainly by genital-to-genital contact, playing leap-frog from one sexual partner to the other. But they can be spread in other ways: sharing towels, bathing suits, gym outfits. Sleeping bags should always be aired after use, as the lice and nits hide in the quilting.

This is one disease you *can* get from a toilet, so don't put your bottom on a public toilet seat.

• ▲ •

Do I have to go to the doctor if I have crabs, or can I treat them myself?

You can treat them yourself, but you must be thorough. Go to a drug store, ask the pharmacist for a bottle of Kwellada lotion or shampoo, and use as directed. For the next four days, you *must* also wash your jeans, gym outfits, pyjamas, underwear, sheets, towels—everything that's been in contact with your skin—to get rid of the crabs and nits. Your sexual partner must also follow the same routine.

A few don'ts:

- Don't shave your pubic hair. There will always be a few crabs who "head for the hills" and hide in the hair between the genitals and the anus.
- Don't take a boiling hot bath in order to "cook" or drown them.
- Don't use any insecticide to try to kill them.

• ▲ •

If I'm using birth control, am I protected against STDs and HIV (AIDS virus)?

The birth-control pill, an IUD (intra-uterine contraceptive device) and the rhythm method offer *no* protection against STDs and HIV (AIDS virus). Anyone using these methods of birth control should also use condoms lubricated with spermicide, and foam for protection against STDs and HIV. But, even condoms and foam offer only limited protection against herpes and genital warts.

6

Don't Take Chances:
Birth Control

Most kids know about birth control but many do not use it—especially the first time they have sex. Here are some of the reasons kids have given me for not using birth control. None of them are valid.

- "I didn't think we'd go all the way."
- "Birth control makes it seem planned. It's not spontaneous."
- "My boy-friend (or girl-friend) doesn't want to."
- "We don't do it often enough."
- "It was the first time so I didn't think I could get pregnant."
- "My parents would find out."

Unless you want to get pregnant, there are *no* excuses for not using birth control. It's amazing but, one in ten females attending high school get pregnant before they graduate. One in ten! That's high! So if you're going to have sex, you have to use birth control. It's as simple as that.

What is the absolute best method of birth control?

The best method of birth control is still the word "NO."
It is the only method that is 100 percent effective. It
makes life easier in lots of ways:

- You never have to worry about getting
  pregnant, getting sexually transmitted diseases
  (STDs) or HIV (AIDS virus).
- Deciding in advance that your answer is "NO"
  means you don't have to wrestle with the
  question of whether you want to have sex with a
  given person on any given evening. So much
  simpler.
- It spares you the heartache of possibly feeling
  had, used or manipulated.
- "Abstinence makes the heart grow fonder." If
  virginity is important to you, and you believe
  that sex should be for marriage only, then you
  can be proud of yourself for living up to your
  convictions.
- Unlike condoms, pills, foam, etc., the word "NO"
  is free. You can't use it up, either.
- Your parents will be delighted and relieved.

There is a lot of peer pressure on teens today to be
involved in sex, so saying "NO" isn't always easy. But
the fact remains that all other methods of birth control
carry some risk of unwanted pregnancy. And the risk of
contracting a sexually transmitted disease—including
HIV (AIDS virus)—has never been greater. Good reasons
to say "NO"—and stick to your guns.

•   ▲   •

I've heard you can't get pregnant the first time you have sex. Is this true?

No, it is not true! Sperm don't know it's your first time, and they aren't keeping score.

This is only one of the non-methods of birth control I hear about from kids. Unfortunately this kind of misinformation results in many an unplanned pregnancy. Here are some other common questions about pregnancy:

Can you get pregnant if the female does not have an orgasm? Yes. Again, sperm don't know or care whether or not either of you had an orgasm; that's your problem. They just want to get there.

Can you get pregnant if you're menstruating? Theoretically you shouldn't get pregnant; but some females have been known to ovulate, and get pregnant, during their period. So don't count on this as a method of birth control.

Can you get pregnant if you have sex with your eyes open? Yup. Eyes open or eyes shut, you can get pregnant if you don't use birth control.

Can you get pregnant if you douche right after sex? Some kids believe that if they use water, or cola, or beer to wash out the vagina immediately after sex, this will kill or remove the sperm. But in fact, this may push them up into the cervix, and actually *increase* the possibility of pregnancy.

If I take one *birth-control pill, will I get pregnant?* The birth-control pill works *only* if you take them as prescribed. So popping one pill just before you "do it" won't protect you from pregnancy.

Can you use plastic wrap as a condom? Plastic wrap was designed to keep air out, not sperm in. Also, don't try to use a plastic sandwich bag, the corner of a green garbage bag with a twist tie, or the wrapper from a loaf of bread. Use a brand-name condom, and use it properly (see page 68).

Can you get pregnant if he pulls out before he shoots? Yes. Withdrawal of the penis, or pulling out, before ejaculation is not a method of birth control. Even if he does pull out in time, the lubrication ("pre-cum") that appears at the tip of the penis when the male is sexually aroused does contain some sperm. If this lubrication comes into contact with his partner's genitals, she can get pregnant.

Can you get pregnant if he cums between your legs? Yes, you can. Sperm, deposited anywhere on the mucous membranes of the female genitals, can swim —into the vagina, up through the cervix, into the uterus and Fallopian tubes—and POW, you're preggers. So, it's possible to do everything but intercourse and still end up pregnant.

There are two kinds of birth control: the kind that works and the kind that doesn't. If you're going to be sexually active, you must use an effective method of birth control. See your doctor, or go to a birth-control clinic (see the Directory at the back of this book), to find out which method is best for you.

• ▲ •

Can you get pregnant if you don't take your panties off?

No. Sperm can be very determined, but they can't penetrate fabric.

One form of sexual arousal is called "dry humping" by kids. The male, with his clothes on, lies on top of the female, who also has her clothes on, and together they imitate intercourse. Often this leads to the male ejaculating in his shorts. While this won't lead to pregnancy, I'm still concerned because if you're involved in this kind of activity it won't be long before you go all the way. Then you *could* get pregnant.

So, talk about it with your boy-friend and have a method of birth control handy just in case . . .

•   ▲   •

Is there another method of birth control I can use?

Instructions for the rhythm method and other "natural" methods of birth control that do not require taking pills or using "foreign objects" are complicated. For this reason, it is better to have them explained to you in person by a birth control counsellor. Phone your local Family Planning or birth-control clinic to make an appointment.

These natural methods of birth control are based on your not having sex when you are ovulating and they will work only if your menstrual cycle is regular and predictable. Many teenagers have unpredictable cycles, making the failure rate for natural methods unacceptably high. So this is a form of birth control that I do not recommend for teens.

•   ▲   •

*Is it safe to have sex without birth control if you do it
right before or right after your period?*

There is no really safe time for teens. If you're going to
have sex, you must use birth control.

As well, sex without condoms and foam at any time
of the month puts you at risk for STDs and the HIV
(AIDS virus) unless you are in a long-term, monoga-
mous relationship. So don't take chances—get a good
method of birth control.

•   ▲   •

*Is it okay to let a guy finger you? Can you get preg-
nant?*

There is a slight risk of pregnancy by fingering. When a
guy is aroused, he lubricates. And since there are sperm
in this lubrication, if he touches his penis and then
fingers his partner, sperm will be deposited in her vagina and she can become pregnant.

Anyone involved in fingering needs to understand
that sexual intercourse is most likely the next step. If
you've reached this point, it's time for the two of you to
stop, talk about it and get a good method of birth
control, such as condoms and foam, rather than risk an
unplanned pregnancy, STDs and HIV (AIDS).

•   ▲   •

*Where do I go to get birth control? Do I have to have a
physical exam? Will they tell my parents?*

There are several places you can go. Make an appointment with the doctor (for a time when you are not

menstruating). Some females are embarrassed talking to their family doctor, who has known them and their parents for years, about birth control. If you are embarrassed, find another doctor or make an appointment at a birth-control clinic. Under the rules of confidentiality, doctors are not supposed to inform your parents that you've requested birth control.

At the clinic, they will take your weight, blood pressure and a sample of urine. They will ask if you have ever had sex before. Please be honest—they're not being snoopy; they need to know. You will also be asked about your personal and family medical history.

They will discuss all methods of birth control so that you can make an informed choice. Whatever method you choose, you'll be shown how to use it properly.

Whether or not you have a pelvic exam depends on the doctor or the policies of the clinic. If you've never had sex before, in all probability they won't do a pelvic exam, but if you have, they will want to check for STDs. A pelvic exam isn't a big deal (see page 26).

Making the decision to get birth control and then going for it are the hardest parts—after that, it's a breeze. It's a great idea to take your boy-friend with you. He needs to know everything too and he is as responsible for birth control as you are.

•　▲　•

I do need birth control, but I'm terrified my parents will find it.

You're not alone. Even if you have wonderful, supportive, loving parents, they may be reluctant to discuss birth control, convinced that if they do they are giving you permission to be sexually active, even encouraging you. And some parents are not elated to learn that their "baby" is involved in sex.

While most parents would prefer that you use birth control rather than risk pregnancy, STDs and HIV (AIDS virus), don't expect them to stand up on the kitchen table and cheer when they find out.

You know your parents, and if you are convinced that they would be very angry, upset, disappointed or disapproving, find a hiding place for your contraceptives: your purse (if that is off-limits to your family); the pocket of an out-of-season jacket hanging in your closet; a book jammed in the bookcase; the toe of a pair of leg-warmers or bulky knee-socks. I'm sure you can think of a secret spot where foam, condoms, a diaphragm or pills would go undiscovered.

When you're more comfortable with your decision to use birth control, perhaps you'll discuss it with your parents. That way you won't have the feeling you are sneaking around.

• ▲ •

Sue, you're always talking about condoms and foam. My boyfriend and I have decided to use them. We know how to use a condom but we're not sure how to use the foam.

Couples like you make my day. You've chosen a good method of birth control—condoms and foam together give 99.9 percent protection, as effective as the birth-control pill. They will also help protect you from STDs and HIV (AIDS virus). I'm impressed.

Contraceptive foam is a spermicide: it kills sperm instantly on contact. It comes in a vial and looks like whipping cream (but do *not* use whipping cream, shaving cream or hair mousse). Before you have sex, while he's rolling on the condom (see page 68 for instructions on how to use a condom) shake the container, place the applicator over the tip of the vial and gently push down. Release the pressure before the applicator is full, and don't remove it immediately or the foam will spray all over you. Then remove the applicator and insert it into the vagina as high up as it will go—it won't hurt. Press the plunger to deposit all the foam high up around the cervix. It's important that you do this ten to fifteen minutes before sex—not early in the evening before a concert or movie.

You may want to insert it *after* oral-genital sex, though, because the foam has a distinctive flavour.

Foam is absorbed by the vagina after about half an hour. So if you have sex again later in the evening, use another condom and another applicator of foam for protection.

Contraceptive foam is available on the open shelves in most drug stores. You won't have to ask for it. It's a good idea to buy some and practise using it alone, before you have sex with your boyfriend.

• ▲ •

How does the birth-control pill work? How do I use it?

The birth-control pill is probably the most reliable method of birth control—99.9 percent effective if taken as prescribed. The pill prevents ovulation—no ovulation, no pregnancy.

There are several different brands of birth-control

pill. Instructions on how to take the pill may vary, depending on the brand, so please be very clear about how to use the brand you are given. Make sure you understand the instructions before you leave the birth-control clinic or doctor's office. If you have any questions, feel free to phone them.

During the first month that you take the pill, use a back-up method such as condoms and foam. The pill may not protect against pregnancy until the second month that you take it.

• ▲ •

What are the good and bad side effects of the birth-control pill?

In brief, here are the good effects:

- You're using the best non-permanent method of birth control available today.
- Your periods are regular, lighter and shorter, with usually no cramps.
- Your acne may clear up—generally within three months. (If it doesn't, go back to the doctor and request another brand of pill.)

There are a few mild side effects:

- You may gain about five pounds when you first go on the pill. This is normal. Anything more than five pounds is just plain fat and means you need to exercise and cut down on calories.
- Your breasts may be fuller than usual and tender. This will probably last only three months.

- Sometimes acne gets worse. See your doctor.
- Some females find the pill lowers their sex drive, or libido. If so, ask to change to another brand of pill.
- You may feel some nausea. Try taking the pill with your big meal of the day. If this does not work, see your doctor, who will change your brand.

There are also *serious side effects* to watch for:

- Severe abdominal pain
- Severe chest pain or shortness of breath
- Severe headaches
- Blurred vision
- Severe leg pain.

If you notice *any* of these signs, call your doctor or go to the hospital emergency department without delay.

REMEMBER:
- The pill alone will not protect you against STDs or the HIV (AIDS virus). You must also use a condom and foam.

There are some females who should not take the pill: women over thirty-five; smokers; anyone with a personal or family history of heart disease, liver disease, high blood pressure, varicose veins or migraine headaches. In these cases your doctor will advise an alternative method of birth control. If you're diabetic and want to take the pill you should see your doctor for insulin adjustment.

The birth-control pill does *not* cause cancer. In fact,

current studies indicate that females who have taken the pill show a lower incidence of uterine cancer.

•   ▲   •

Can I continue to smoke if I take the birth-control pill?

No! Smoking is out. We know that the risks of heart attacks and strokes increase dramatically for smokers who are taking the pill. An occasional cigarette at a party won't hurt, but if you smoke more than half a pack a day you are at risk, and should certainly give up smoking before you go on the pill. It's not worth taking the chance.

•   ▲   •

Help! I missed a pill. What should I do?

If you forget to take the pill at your regular time, but remember within four hours, you should still take it. If you remember the following day, then remove the missed pill from the package and take the next pill at the regular time. If you miss two pills, remove them from the package and take the next pill at your usual time. In either case, you must use a back-up method of birth control, such as condoms and foam, during the rest of that package.

If you miss three pills, forget it. (You'll probably get your period.) Back to square one. Dig out your instructions on how to start taking the pill and begin a new pack on your regular starting day. Again, you *must* use a back-up method of birth control during that entire package.

If you've missed taking more than one pill and aren't sure what to do, phone your local birth control or family planning clinic.

• ▲ •

I am on the birth-control pill and I've never missed taking even one. But I didn't get my last period. Does this mean I'm pregnant?

If you don't get a period, but haven't missed any pills, don't panic—you're not pregnant, you're fine. There was probably not enough build-up in the uterus to come away as menstruation, and you're experiencing a "silent period." Not to worry. If you're on the 28-day pill, continue; if you're on the 21-day pill, start a fresh pack of pills on the next Sunday as you normally would.

If you miss two periods, check it out with your doctor or clinic. They will probably do a simple test to rule out the possibility of pregnancy, and then tell you to carry on with your routine.

• ▲ •

The pills are so expensive! Where can I get them cheaper?

Good point. Yup, the pill is expensive—but cheaper than an unplanned pregnancy. There are places where you can get the pill cheaper, but they're not always easy to find.

- Some birth-control clinics sell the pill at a reduced rate.

- Small, independent local druggists often charge less than big chain stores. Always phone around before you have your prescription filled.
- If you find you are temporarily broke, let's say at Christmas time, ask your family doctor or clinic for a couple of free packs. They will give you enough to tide you over.
- If your parents know you are on the pill and they have a drug plan through their employers, ask them if it covers you. If so, you could get your pills this way.
- Similarly, if your parents are on welfare or unemployment insurance, you can get birth control pills much cheaper.
- Don't forget your boy-friend. You're sharing the benefits of birth control; why shouldn't you share the cost?

My concern is that you might go off the pill just because you're broke. This could mess up your cycle for a few months, and you might end up pregnant.

• ▲ •

My boy-friend has offered to buy my birth-control pills because I can't afford them. Somehow I feel uncomfortable about this.

You are one lucky lady to have a boy-friend who is so considerate of you and your finances. I'm impressed that he is willing to do his share and take partial responsibility for your mutual concern—contraception.

But I can understand that you might feel uncomfortable if your boy-friend paid for the pills. Are you afraid this may alter your relationship? Even if he does pay, you don't lose the right to say, "No, not tonight." Does it make you feel inadequate that you can't afford your own pills? There are lots of possibilities. You need to focus on your feelings of discomfort, and then judge whether or not they're rational. If they aren't, then discard them.

I know many teenage couples where the boy-friend is happy to pay for the pills (some even phone the pharmacy for a refill and pick them up). Others take turns paying. Maybe you'd be more comfortable with an arrangement like that. Talk it over with your partner. It sounds like you're both rational and mature, with good communication and a high level of trust between you. So I'm sure you'll be able to work this one out.

• ▲ •

Will the pill affect my ability to have kids in the future?

It's difficult to give a definite reply, but current studies suggest you will probably not have difficulty becoming pregnant when you decide you want to be a mother.

Some women have experienced problems in conceiving after being on the pill for a period of time, but these difficulties may not have been pill-related. These women may never have ovulated, or may have a blockage in their Fallopian tubes, or their vaginal secretions may kill sperm.

In fact, many women become pregnant within a month or two of stopping the pill.

• ▲ •

I have been on the pill for four years and my doctor now recommends that I go off it to give my body a rest.

When the pill first appeared, it contained very high levels of hormones, and doctors recommended that women "rest" from it for six months every two years. Unfortunately this rest frequently results in unplanned pregnancies.

Now the dosage has been drastically reduced so that the risks and side effects are minimal. Informed physicians do not recommend a rest from the birth-control pill.

So unless you are experiencing pill-related problems and your doctor takes you off, stay on the pill.

You might wish to discuss this with another doctor, or go to a birth-control clinic.

• ▲ •

My doctor put me on tetracycline for an infection. She warned me that my pill might not be effective, and told me to use a back-up method. Is this true?

Absolutely. Whenever you are given any prescription, tell your doctor you're on the pill, and make sure it's okay to take the two together. In the case of antibiotics, you must use a back-up method of birth control, such as condoms and foams.

• ▲ •

Is there a birth-control pill for guys?

No. At the present time the only method of birth control that males can use is sterilization or condoms. But remember, a condom alone is not the most effective method of birth control. For the best possible protection against STDs, HIV (AIDS virus) and pregnancy, the female should also use contraceptive foam.

• ▲ •

What is a diaphragm? Where do I get it? How effective is it? Why don't more people use it?

Wow—am I ever glad you're asking all these questions. A diaphragm is a small rubber dome, fitted over a spring-type circular ring. It acts as a barrier to prevent sperm from passing into the cervix. If you're thinking of getting a diaphragm, be sure to have one fitted by your doctor or at a birth-control clinic. You will be shown how to insert and remove it, and then you should practise a few times until you're sure of how to use it correctly.

A diaphragm *must* be used with a spermicidal gel. You spread this around the rim, and put a small amount inside and outside the dome. Pinch opposite sides of the rim together, then slide the diaphragm into the vagina and up until it fit snugly and comfortably over the cervix. Check the fit by inserting one finger into the vagina and running it round the rim. If the diaphragm is inserted properly, you won't even know it's there, nor will your partner.

A diaphragm can be inserted up to two hours before you have sex, and *must* be left in for at least eight hours afterward to ensure all the sperm have been killed by the gel. If you have sex more than once, you must insert additional spermicidal foam or gel.

To remove, insert one finger into the vagina and hook it onto the rim of the diaphragm. Gently pull the diaphragm down and out. It should be washed, dried and powdered with cornstarch after use. Store it in its container in a cool place.

The diaphragm is supposed to be 95 percent effective, but the failure rate can be higher if you don't insert it correctly and use a spermicide *every* time you have sex. Many kids don't like the diaphragm because it's messier and less convenient than some other methods, like the pill or condoms and foam, which are more "user-friendly."

• ▲ •

What is an IUD? Can kids get one?

IUD stands for intra-uterine device. It is a foreign body inserted into the uterus to prevent a fertilized egg from being implanted.

The IUD is not recommended for females who have never been pregnant, who have heavy menstrual periods with severe cramps, or who have a number of sexual partners. If you have an IUD there's also a greater risk of PID (Pelvic Inflammatory Disease) which could cause permanent sterility. For these reasons IUDs are not usually recommended for teenagers.

• ▲ •

Last night my girl-friend and I were having sex and the condom broke. We stopped right away but I'm scared. What should we have done?

Yup, condoms do break occasionally. There may have been a manufacturing defect, or perhaps you didn't put the condom on properly (see page 68).

I do hope you and your girl-friend were using foam at the same time; since a condom alone is not the most effective method of birth control, condoms and foam should be used together every time you have sex. If the condom does break, it's advisable to insert an additional applicator full of foam into the vagina to provide extra protection.

If less than seventy-two hours (three days) has gone by since the condom broke, you and your girl-friend can go to your doctor or a family-planning clinic and inquire about the "morning-after pill." But if over seventy-two hours have passed, all you can do is wait till her next period is due. If it doesn't come, she should have a pregnancy test.

This is a scary situation. To prevent it from happening again, be sure to use name-brand condoms that are prelubricated with spermicide. And use them properly.

• ▲ •

I heard there is a pill you can take after sex to prevent a pregnancy. Where can I get it?

The "morning-after pill" is not one pill but a series of four pills taken at specific times to prevent an unplanned pregnancy. They contain high doses of synthetic hormones that prevent a fertilized egg from implanting itself in the lining of the uterus. Because the morning-after pill is hard on your system, it is not used as a routine method of birth control—only in emergency or crisis situations, such as sexual assault (rape), unplanned, unprotected sexual contact, or cases of contraceptive failure (such as a burst condom, or a diaphragm slipping out of place).

You must go to your doctor or nearest birth-control

clinic *within seventy-two hours* after sex. The counsellor needs to know the exact date your last menstrual period started in order to evaluate the possibility of pregnancy. If you had sex mid-cycle (the time of ovulation), you will be given four pills—two to be taken at eight o'clock at night and two to be taken at eight o'clock the next morning. Since the hormones may cause severe nausea, take an anti-nausea pill (such as Gravol) twenty minutes before.

If more than seventy-two hours has passed since you had sex, conception may already have taken place, and the morning-after pill will not work. If you are pregnant and take the morning-after pill, there is a good chance that the drug will cause a congenital abnormality in the baby. For this reason it is essential that you be honest about the date you had sex.

Your period should come within the next month. If it doesn't come, have a pregnancy test every week until menstruation begins. Avoid sexual contact until you get a good method of birth control.

The morning-after pill is *not* considered a method of birth control.

●   ▲   ●

I am seventeen years old and I want to be sterilized. I know I do not want to have a baby, not ever. Can I be sterilized at my age?

I am constantly amazed at the conviction in statements like yours. Although I feel that kids usually have a good sense of what they want in life, things change; nothing is carved in stone. And because sterilization is considered permanent, most medical professionals would be reluctant to sterilize someone your age. So having a tubal ligation (for females) or a vasectomy (for males) really takes determination.

Your family doctor would refer you to a specialist, either a gynaecologist or a urologist. This specialist, in turn, would insist on a psychiatric evaluation to be sure you understand the consequences of your decision. Based on the psychiatrist's recommendation, the specialist would decide whether or not to proceed with your sterilization. Please don't expect it to happen the day after tomorrow—for after you are approved, you may have to wait up to a year for the operation. Until then, use a good method of birth control.

And don't forget—even if you've been sterilized, you still must use a condom and foam to protect against STDs and HIV (AIDS virus).

7

The First Time

STOP
RIGHT
HERE

Before you go any further, be *sure* that you and your partner have read Chapters 4, 5, and 6, about AIDS, Sexually Transmitted Diseases and Birth Control.

The first time you have intercourse is special. You want it to be good—the best—because you will remember it always.

Just as you plan and prepare for any big occasion, so it should be with sex.

Think about what you want from a relationship: love, trust and caring; good, intimate communication; commitment. Don't settle for less—it's what you deserve.

When you plan your romantic scenario, make sure you have plenty of uninterrupted time, soft lighting, good music, a comfortable setting—everything you want. But there is also another, less romantic side to sex, things you *must* discuss with your partner beforehand.

Talk about your anxieties: not doing it right, your

body, your partner's body, even the possibility of failure. Talk about your fears of AIDS and sexually transmitted diseases, unplanned pregnancy, the risks and the protection you will both use. It's not easy to talk about such things, I know, but it is essential.

And be prepared to laugh. Sex is funny; at times it's an absolute hoot. Enjoy.

•   ▲   •

How do I know if we are getting involved in a sexual relationship?

Wow, this is something we as parents lecture and preach about, especially to our daughters, but "Don't let any guy touch you between the neck and the knees" is not really sex education.

Let's look at the courtship procedure. It starts out by meeting someone you like, getting to know them, holding hands, touching, hugging, kissing and necking. Feels good, and is so very nice. If the necking continues it leads to French kissing. Kids call this open mouth kissing, tonguing, "Frenching," deep throat. If French kissing continues it can lead to petting on top of your clothes. This is very sexually stimulating for both partners, and before long it can lead to petting under your clothes. Then the clothes come off and the next stage is oral sex and/or sexual intercourse.

This courtship procedure is as old as the hills; you did not invent it. But now you know exactly what is going to happen and when. So, you have to decide if that is what you *want* to happen. How do you feel about nude petting at this stage of your life? Are you ready for sex, because once you get started, it is very difficult to stop and if you don't stop early enough before you know it, it is too late.

So where do you draw the line? Well, I am firmly convinced the French kissing is the cut-off point. Sorry about that, and I know I do sound like your mother, but French kissing is really asking permission. It is a guy saying to a girl, "Do you like me, do you like what I am doing, shall I continue?"

If the female returns the French kisses, she is saying, "I like you, I like what you are doing, you are doing just fine, carry on big boy." Is this the message you want to convey? If not, stop at French kissing. You know where this is leading, and if you're not ready for it, say so. Stop right there and go for a walk, or play Trivial Pursuit rather than Sexual Pursuit.

This almost sounds as though it is always the guy who is the mover and instigator. But females can also be very assertive and demanding and make it very embarrassing for a *guy* to say no. I have heard guys say that females will question their masculinity if they won't go further. This can be very difficult for a male. The expectation that he has an "ever-ready penis" and wants to do it anytime, any place and with anybody is wrong.

Now, if you are older, in a stable, long-term committed relationship, have talked about sexual activity and both of you have agreed that you are ready for it and that it is an integral part of your loving relationship, then read the rest of this chapter, go slowly, relax and enjoy.

• ▲ •

My boy-friend wants to have sex, and although I love

him very much, I'm not sure I'm ready for that. How will I know when I am?

I'm impressed that you have thought about this. Let's look at some of the things you might want to consider in making this important decision.

For starters, why do you want to have sex? Here are some reasons that might push you into a sexual relationship before *you* are ready:

Your boy-friend wants to have sex. Lines like, "You would if you loved me" and "Prove your love," may manipulate you into doing something you don't really want. What makes him happy will not necessarily make you happy.

You think sex will help you keep him. You're afraid that if you won't "do it" he'll find someone else who will. If he loves you, he'll be willing to wait.

Peer pressure. All your friends seem to be "doing it." You feel you must be the only virgin in the whole school. Please believe me—you're not. Lots of teens are in the same situation.

To prove your femininity. You don't have to have sex with guys to convince yourself and others that you are attractive, capable of getting and keeping a guy.

To "get even" with your parents. "Doing it" with a guy because you're angry at your parents and you want to rebel, or doing something you know would upset them, are not valid reasons for having sex.

Curiosity. Everybody talks about sex and you feel you are missing out on something good. Yeah, sex can be great—provided you know what you're doing, feel ready for it and are protected against unplanned pregnancies and all STDs.

Now let's turn to the positive side. You love your boyfriend; do you feel he loves you? Is he committed to the relationship? Would you stay together even if you decided not to have sex? Do you feel good about the relationship? Can you talk about sex openly and comfortably together? If the answer to all these questions is yes, it sounds like the makings of a loving, caring, committed relationship. Sex could add a whole new dimension to it. But if you still don't feel good about "going all the way," don't do it.

If you decide to have sex, then you will need to discuss:

- Which method of birth control will be effective and acceptable to both of you. Who will provide it?
- How you would handle an unwanted pregnancy —because no method of birth control is 100 percent effective (except the word "NO").
- Your boy-friend's previous sexual experiences, if any, and the use of a condom to protect against sexually transmitted diseases (STDs) and HIV (AIDS).
- You and your boy-friend's willingness to abstain from sex with other partners.
- How your parents would react if they found out you were having sex. Could you handle that?
- How you would feel about your decision to have sex if your relationship were to break up.

Since there is no sure way to tell if you are ready for a sexual relationship, thinking and talking about these points will help clarify your feelings. It sounds to me like you and your boy-friend communicate well and he isn't pressuring you into a hasty decision. So go slow.

If you decide you're not ready, don't feel you have to apologize, justify or defend your decision. This is an important first in your life; do what's right for you.

• ▲ •

Exactly what happens with intercourse? Everyone in the world seems to know all about it but me.

It only seems that way. Believe me, lots of kids talk about it without ever having done it; it takes more guts to ask.

Usually, before intercourse, a couple will become sexually aroused by necking, French kissing and petting. This is called foreplay and can last as long as you like. The guy will probably get an erection; her genitals will be swollen and throbbing. At this point, the male should roll on a condom and the female should insert the foam.

So far, so good. Now the male, gently and slowly at first, starts to thrust or push his penis in, with an in-and-out movement. The female moves her pelvis up and down in rhythm with his thrusting. As the speed and depth of the thrusting increase, their sexual excitement increases till the male ejaculates. The female may experience orgasm anywhere along the line, or later with clitoral stimulation.

There are a variety of positions the couple may assume. A few are described below:

The missionary position. The female lies on her back with legs spread; the male is on his hands and knees on top of her and inserts his penis in her vagina. This is the most common position, and it offers the advantage of face-to-face contact—the couple can kiss, fondle and cuddle.

Side by side, facing each other. The female's bottom leg is straight while she hooks her top leg snugly around her partner's hip. This position does not allow the penis to penetrate the vagina as deeply, and may be more comfortable for the female than the missionary position. There are many ways to change the angle of entry—what I call the angle of dangle.

Doggie style, or Fido and Fifi. The female kneels on all fours while the male inserts his penis into her vagina from behind. This position allows the male to stroke his partner's clitoris and breasts while she reaches back and strokes his testicles.

Female on top. The male lies on his back and the female kneels or sits on her heels and places her partner's penis in her vagina. In the beginning, the female may feel shy or embarrassed because she is so visible, but that's part of the turn-on. In this position she can control the depth of penetration while her partner can stimulate her breasts and clitoris.

Got it? Close your eyes and imagine how it all fits. You'll probably find that you become sexually aroused just thinking about it. That's okay, normal, natural— and fun.

• ▲ •

How can you tell if a girl is aroused?

I hate to think of you with pencil and check-list, but here are some of the signs:

- Her breathing may change, and she may sigh, moan or gasp.
- Her lips become fuller; her pupils dilate.
- An uneven redness, or blush, may appear on her breasts and upper chest.
- She may feel restless, squirming, antsy, and she may thrust her pelvis forward.
- Her nipples may become erect and firm— "poky."
- During petting, she may say, "Ooh, that feels good," or, "Oh, I like that," perhaps gently moving your hand to show you exactly how and where she likes to be touched.
- She may shift her body so that you can touch her genitals more easily.
- Her genitals will be swollen, warm and wet, or lubricated.
- Her clitoris fills with blood and, like the penis, becomes erect.

The signs of sexual arousal vary from person to person and from time to time. A female can be really turned on and not have all of the above going on. Don't worry— she'll probably let you know.

•   ▲   •

How can you tell if a guy is excited? Is heavy breathing a sign?

Usually the bulge in his jeans is a dead giveaway—he gets an erection. This can happen during masturbation, necking, petting or fantasizing about sex.

The other signs of sexual arousal in males closely resemble those of females: flushed skin, fuller lips, dilated pupils, poky nipples, heavy breathing and pelvic thrusting.

• ▲ •

Last night we were necking and my boy-friend got really horny. I didn't want to go any further, but when I refused to have sex, he got mad and said it was my fault, I gave him the hard-on, he was uncomfortable and I had to do something about it.

Why do *you* have to do something about it? He has the problem, not you; you are fine. Granted, if he's aroused, he may feel some pressure in his genitals. But surely he's used to having erections by now and knows he can't have sex every time his penis stands at attention. What does he do when you're not there?

Males know that the slight congestion caused by an unfulfilled erection is easily relieved by masturbating. You might suggest he go to the bathroom and look after it himself—it's not a big deal. He may have an erection because of you, but you don't have to do anything about it.

Now that you know you are capable of turning him on, better think twice before you allow it to happen again. It's not fair to "tease" him when you know he responds this way. Make it very clear how far you're willing to go. He should respect that, and you should stick to it.

• ▲ •

How do I get a girl hot?

I assume you're asking about the erogenous zones—areas of the body that are responsive to sexual stimulation. In both sexes, the erogenous zones include the ears, the neck, lips, breasts, genitals and the inner surfaces of the wrists and thighs. But the truth is that your whole body is one humungous erogenous zone, from head to toe. Your skin is the biggest sex organ you have. So if someone you find attractive touches you *anywhere*—your hand, foot or hair—you practically flip out.

Some people are turned on by back rubs, foot massages, sucking fingers or toes—you name it. No two people are alike, so do not limit yourself to the so-called erogenous zones. Getting there is half the fun. Experiment together, ask your partner what feels good, and be sure to tell her what you like, too.

But if a female is not attracted to you nothing you do is going to turn her on. Better luck next time.

• ▲ •

Does it hurt girls to have sex the first time?

Nope, not necessarily. A female who has never had sex may have a thin membrane, called the hymen, partially covering the vaginal opening. When this membrane is stretched, there may be some discomfort and bleeding. For some females, this happens during their first experience of sexual intercourse. Others may stretch or rupture the hymen by using tampons, engaging in active sports, "heavy petting" or "fingering."

Sexual intercourse is usually more comfortable and enjoyable for both partners once the hymen is stretched enough to allow the penis to penetrate, or enter, the vagina easily. It helps if you're both relaxed and ready, comfortable with your partner and your decision to have sex. A good method of birth control, such as condoms and foam, will lessen anxiety about unplanned pregnancy or STD and HIV (AIDS).

Plan it out, making sure you have privacy and time to relax and enjoy. Cuddle, hug, kiss and stroke each other. Don't focus solely on the genitals, but everywhere your partner likes to be touched. As sexual arousal increases, the female genitals become lubricated, and this clear mucous secretion will make penetration easier.

You should be using a condom that is prelubricated with spermicide. If extra lubrication is necessary, a water-based gel such as Lubafax, available from any drug store, may be applied to the condom. Do *not* use petroleum jelly, which can weaken the condom and cause it to break.

Even with plenty of lubrication, the vaginal opening may be tight simply because she's a bit tense. If so, then gently, Bently! Go slow. Change positions so that penetration is not as deep. A good way is to lie side by side facing each other, with the female's top leg hooked over her partner's hip.

If intercourse is still uncomfortable, stop. The hymen may be unusually thick, the vagina may be irritated, or there may be some other problem which should be checked by a doctor before having sex again.

• ▲ •

If you have done many sexual things but never gone all the way, are you still a virgin?

A virgin is someone who has never experienced penile penetration. So you can do "everything but"—which means you can engage in masturbation, heavy-duty petting, oral-genital sex, and still be technically a "virgin."

This brings up another point: namely, the value of virginity. If you believe that it is important for you to "save yourself" and remain "pure" for your husband or wife, then hang on to it. It is important, and valid. If both partners abstain from sex before marriage, there is a greatly reduced risk of contracting HIV (AIDS virus) or any other STD—not to mention an accidental pregnancy.

My main concern is that teenagers who do "everything but" will get carried away in the heat of passion and have sex without adequate protection. Don't ever let sex "just happen."

By the way, if you haven't had sex but you use tampons you are still definitely a virgin.

•　▲　•

Can a doctor tell if you are a virgin during a pelvic exam?

No. In doing a pelvic exam, a doctor will see if the hymen has stretched, or ruptured, but will not be able to tell whether this is the result of having intercourse, using tampons, or genital petting.

•　▲　•

How can you tell if a boy is a virgin or not?

You can't—which is fortunate for guys who are "all talk and no action." Although many young males are virgins, few will admit to it, since it's considered cool to be experienced and to have scored any number of times. This attitude only increases the pressure on young males to have sex, perhaps before they are ready for it.

For males and females alike, it does not matter what everybody else is doing—or what they say they're doing. Believe me, there are a lot more virgins out there than you think. What is important is that you feel good about yourself and your reasons for choosing to have, or not to have, sex.

• ▲ •

I'm an eighteen-year-old guy. I've never "done it" and I'm terrified I won't know what to do.

Most guys feel exactly the same way. The first time is as important and scary for a male as for a female. In fact, he may feel more anxiety than his partner, because there is a myth that males must always be knowledgeable, skilful and in control in sexual situations. This can be pretty stressful for a guy who's never "done it" before, especially if he is reluctant to reveal his lack of experience to his partner.

You weren't an instant expert the first time you rode a bicycle, and you won't be with sex, either. Sure, the first few times will probably be a little awkward and clumsy, perhaps even embarrassing; they are for most people. But with time and experience the fear will subside, and you'll wonder why you were ever worried.

Let's face it. If you really think about it, sex is pretty comical so it helps if you can see the humour in the situation.

• ▲ •

I had sex for the first time and didn't like it. Is there something wrong?

Some kids say sex is amazing; others say it's the pits. Who is right?

While sex may be perfectly natural, it's not naturally perfect, and the first time can be a real bummer. The stress and anxiety of your first sexual encounter frequently prevents males from achieving a full erection, or they may ejaculate too quickly. You'll survive, but it's devastating to the ego. There may be some discomfort for the female if the hymen is intact, and it is totally unrealistic to expect a cataclysmic orgasm the first time you "do it." Even under the best of conditions, many people come away from their first sexual contact wondering, "Is that all there is?"

It takes time to become comfortable with your body, and then comfortable with your partner's. Once you relax, you will recognize what feels good for each of you. You'll begin to feel a little more confident, and start to have fun.

On the other hand, if sex is something you don't enjoy, then just don't do it—that's okay too.

8

Curiosity & Concerns

Sex is an instinct, an urge that is as natural as breathing and eating. But satisfying, meaningful sex does not just happen; it is a learned response. Many kids tell me that their first sexual encounters were not great experiences. They did not know what to expect, they were not relaxed, confident or comfortable with themselves, with their partner or with the activity. As the relationship progressed, they found they gradually grew to enjoy it.

There may be some aspects of sexual behaviour that you do not enjoy. You may be turned off by the very idea of oral-genital sex or different positions during intercourse. There are many ways to express sexuality, and you don't have to try them all. So if you experience feelings of aversion, gently but firmly tell your partner that you do not want to do that. If your partner tries to talk you into doing something you don't want to do ("Everybody does it," "Don't be a prude"), then it's time to look at the quality of the relationship. In a truly loving relationship, one partner does not manipulate, coerce, exploit or threaten the other. There is respect for each other's level of sexual comfort.

I hope that, in reading this book, you will learn the different aspects of a sexual relationship. Think about them, but if you decide something is not right for you, then don't do it. It's your body, and your right.

• ▲ •

Is it true that peanut butter, celery and oysters make you horny?

They won't make you horny, but they might make you fat. Many foods are thought to be aphrodisiacs—substances that arouse sexual desire. In fact, they don't do a thing. But since 99 percent of sexual arousal occurs between your ears, these foods, as well as any others you enjoy, *could* turn you on—if you believe they will.

• ▲ •

Is it normal not to want to have sex?

Yes—it is quite normal not to want to be involved in sex for the following reasons:

- Virginity, saving it for marriage, may be important to you.
- You are not ready for it.
- You are scared—of pregnancy, disease, parental reactions or of getting a reputation.
- It is not the kind of relationship you want in your life.
- You are not convinced you are "in love."

If you don't want it, don't do it. It is as simple as that.

• ▲ •

When you get high from drugs or drinking, is it true that you are a better lover?

You may *feel* like a better lover, but it's unlikely your partner would agree. Alcohol lowers your inhibitions but, in fact, it reduces sex drive and the ability to perform. So do drugs. Also, if you are "hammered" or "stoned," you are less likely to practise safer sex.

• ▲ •

How come a guy can only shoot once, while girls can go on and on?

Once a male has ejaculated, there will be a refractory phase during which he loses his erection and no amount of stimulation will produce another one. This may last from minutes to hours, depending on his age, his mood or how tired he is. Generally young males can be re-stimulated to have another erection after a fifteen to thirty minute refractory phase. For older males it takes longer. This is a great opportunity for the male to continue stimulating his partner manually or orally and bring her to orgasm.

Females do not have a refractory phase. If they are highly stimulated they can have multiple orgasms, one after the other in quick succession. Sorry, guys—that's life.

• ▲ •

Am I a sex addict? I really enjoy sex and I feel good about myself for days. Is this normal?

Absolutely. I only wish more people enjoyed their love-making the same way you do. You and your partner obviously have a warm, loving relationship. You feel good about it and each other, so you feel good about yourself. That's the absolute best. Don't worry; you're not addicted to sex. You simply enjoy it.

• ▲ •

I expected sex to be uncomfortable the first few times, but we have been "doing it" for months now, and it still hurts. The skin around my vagina is cracked and raw. Please help. I'm desperate.

It sounds as though you are trying to have intercourse before there was enough vaginal lubrication. Apart from being uncomfortable, this can actually irritate the mucous membrane and may cause small cracks and tears leaving you vulnerable to infection. So have your doctor check it out. During this time, you and your partner should avoid any genital stimulation—no heavy petting, oral sex or intercourse. Give your vagina a rest and a chance to heal. Meanwhile, you can still enjoy lots of hugging, cuddling and snuggling.

Once the problem has been treated and healed, pick up a tube of Lubafax at the drug store to supplement your natural lubrication. And don't try to have sexual intercourse until you are relaxed, aroused and it feels comfortable and pleasurable.

• ▲ •

Whenever my boy-friend and I try to have sex, my vagina tightens up and he can't get his penis in. This is very painful for me, and frustrating for us both.

Ouch! That hurts. It sounds like vaginismus—involuntary spasms of the vaginal muscles that make intercourse difficult, painful or impossible.

A female may develop vaginismus as a result of a bad sexual experience or emotional trauma from a previous relationship. She may have been sexually assaulted (raped); perhaps she was brought up to believe that sex is sinful and "dirty." The very thought of a penis in her vagina triggers vaginal spasms.

Vaginismus is rare among teenagers. But it may have its origins in adolescence and become a major problem later. I strongly recommend that you get some counselling, because the problem will not go away by itself. The counselling consists of examining the relationship, sex education and "homework" exercises designed to relax the vaginal muscles and gradually allow intercourse.

Ask your doctor to refer you to a qualified sex counsellor.

• ▲ •

Can you have sex when you have your period?

There is no physical reason you cannot have sex during menstruation. But in this age of HIV (AIDS virus), it's not advisable because of the increased risk of transmitting the virus.

• ▲ •

Is it possible for a guy to get his "thing" stuck when he's having sex with a girl?

No. You may have got this idea from watching dogs mating—the penis seems to be locked in the female's vagina. Human males sometimes fear this will happen to them during intercourse but it just doesn't happen this way. Human females do not have a sphincter muscle at the opening of the vagina so the penis cannot get trapped.

• ▲ •

I am eighteen, and have recently started having sex with my girl-friend. Every time we try to do it, I can't seem to get it up. I get a semi-erection, not hard enough for intercourse. But when I masturbate, it's just fine. Why won't it work when I want it to?

It's a familiar scenario: you've been out on a great date, you're both feeling mellow, you get into some heavy petting, all systems are "go" and the big moment comes. Then—zap—you loose your erection. Game over, forget it. You are embarrassed, and your girl-friend thinks it's something she did. You go home, and wouldn't you know it—you get the biggest erection of your life. You look at your penis and say, "Where were you when I needed you?!"

Statistics won't comfort you much, but studies indicate that approximately one-half of all males experience occasional episodes of erectile failure—inability to achieve an erection firm enough to enter the vagina. In a very few cases there might be a medical reason; certain medications or poor circulation to the genitals can cause erectile failure. Drugs and alcohol can also inhibit erection. But if you have good erections with masturbation, then not having erections with your girlfriend is more likely caused by stress, anxiety or fear:

- Fear of being inadequate, inexperienced or inept.
- Fear of discovery of sexual activity by parents or peers.
- Fear of STDs and HIV (AIDS virus), a major concern nowadays.
- Fear of rejection or being laughed at.
- Fear of a "trapped" or captive penis.

- Fear of "sinning" or "doing it" against your values.
- Fear that failure indicates homosexuality.

The first thing I would strongly recommend is to abstain from sexual intercourse completely for a while. Sit down and really talk to your girl-friend. Tell her your feelings about what is happening and how you see it affecting you, her and the relationship. She must understand that this problem is not her fault. Agree not to try intercourse for a specific period of time—say, a month. During that time you might do lots of hugging, cuddling, kissing, petting, oral-genital sex, masturbation and mutual masturbation—just no penis in the vagina. This vacation will take the emphasis off performance, and you may find that sex can be perfectly satisfying without intercourse.

Then, very gradually and with no unrealistic expectations, try having intercourse again. If it works, fine; if it doesn't, go back to square one and refrain from intercourse. At this stage, you might consider seeing a sex counsellor, who will help you understand what is happening and why.

Males can be very hard on themselves with regard to their ability to "perform" sex. But loving, caring sex is not a performance. Once you relax and stop worrying about the penis, you may find the problem solves itself.

•   ▲   •

My boy-friend likes to give me a hickey on my neck. I don't like it. My friends tease me, my mom hassles me, and I end up wearing turtle-necks in August. Why does he do it?

A hickey is a bruise. When your partner sucks on your neck, he brings blood vessels to the surface which break and bleed into the surrounding tissues. Red at first, they soon turn purple, then black, and last about two weeks till the blood has been re-absorbed.

Hickeys are not exactly a badge of honour. Just as a dog marks his territory by lifting his leg and squirting on every tree, your boy-friend is marking you as *his* property.

How do you feel about advertising your relationship this way? It seems to me that you have a keen sense of autonomy and have begun to resent this mark of ownership. Personally, I'd like to leave a mark on the end of his nose.

I agree with your mother, and since you don't like his behaviour either, tell him to stop it—now. And if he does it again, don't let him near you till he promises to quit.

• ▲ •

My boy-friend's penis is curved like a hockey stick. When we make love, it hurts me. Is there anything we can do?

If the curve is severe, he may have chordee or Peyronie's disease (see page 10), which only a doctor can diagnose. In any case, the next time you have sex, suggest to him that you experiment with different positions that allow you more control over the angle and depth of penetration of his penis in your vagina—like with you on top, or both of you lying side by side, face to face. Or try rear-entry intercourse, with you resting on your knees and elbows while your boy-friend enters your vagina from behind. This way he can change the angle of insertion so that it is more comfortable for you. Be innovative. Where there's a will, there's a way.

• ▲ •

What is oral sex?

Oral sex or oral-genital sex involves kissing, licking and sucking the genitals. Slang terms include giving head, eating, going down on or giving a blow job. When the male does this to his girl-friend it is called cunnilingus; when the female does it to her boy-friend it is called fellatio. Partners can take turns, or may stimulate each other simultaneously. Oral sex can be used as a means of sexual arousal, but may also bring both partners to orgasm. Oral-genital sex is also part of homosexual love-making.

• ▲ •

What is 69?

Sixty-nine, or *soixante-neuf*, is slang for two people having oral-genital sex at the same time.

• ▲ •

Is oral sex natural? Is it wrong? Do many people do it?

Many couples enjoy oral-genital stimulation as part of their lovemaking. But different people have different ideas of what is natural or unnatural, right or wrong. For some, the thought of putting the mouth "down there" is gross.

If you feel this way, tell your partner. While oral sex can be enjoyable, it's not essential. It does not indicate love. As you become more comfortable with your body and your partner's body, you may feel more comfortable with oral sex, but it may not be right for you just now.

Do not allow anyone to talk you into doing something you are not comfortable with. If you don't want to do it, *don't* do it!

• ▲ •

How do you give a good blow job?

That depends on who's getting it. Personal preferences vary.

Be sure to practise safer sex even when involved in oral-genital activity. Because HIV (AIDS virus) can be found in semen, ejaculate should not be taken into the mouth or a condom can be worn on the penis during oral sex.

Basically, the female takes the head of the penis into her mouth and very gently slides one hand up and down the shaft. Salvia acts as a natural lubricant. She may use her tongue in a flicking motion, varying the intensity of stimulation either to bring on the male's orgasm or to delay it.

What pleases one male will not necessarily be pleasurable for another. The best way to learn how to perform oral-genital sex is to ask your partner what feels good.

• ▲ •

Is there a right and wrong way to give a girl head?

Many females find that oral stimulation of their genitals, especially the clitoris, is less irritating than the manual kind (fingering). The clitoris, like the glans of the penis, is highly sensitive, and too-vigorous stimulation is likely to turn your partner off, not on. The male can use his tongue and lips all around the labia and the vaginal opening, returning to the clitoris occasionally to heighten his partner's pleasure. Some females enjoy having their partner insert one or two fingers into the vagina during cunnilingus.

Again, communication is the key. No one is an instant expert at oral sex. The best way of finding out what pleases your partner is to ask, "Does that feel good?" "Do you like that?"

Because vaginal secretions may contain HIV there is a slight risk of being exposed to the virus during oral-genital sex. You have to decide if you're willing to take that risk. But you must avoid oral-genital sex when your girlfriend has her period or if you have open sores on your mouth because of the increased risk of transmitting the virus.

• ▲ •

What is anal sex?

Anal sex or anal intercourse refers to the insertion of the male's penis into his partner's anus and rectum. While often considered a homosexual act, anal intercourse is also practised by heterosexuals.

Anal intercourse without a condom is an *extremely* high-risk activity for transmitting HIV (AIDS virus). If you do engage in anal sex, you must wear a condom with lots of water soluble lubricant—like K-Y or Lubafax—so that the condom will not break. Do not use petroleum jelly which weakens the condom. And since spermicide can irritate the lining of the rectum, don't use foam or condoms lubricated with spermicide for anal sex. For extra protection, some couples "double-bag it"—that is, they use two condoms, one rolled over the other.

Even with lubrication, the sensitive lining of the rectum may be nicked or torn. If there is any discomfort do not continue.

● ▲ ●

My girl-friend used to really enjoy sex a lot. Now she's just not interested.

In the beginning of a relationship, sexual activity is generally intense and frequent. You can't seem to get enough of each other. In time, the fascination of newness wears off, and the level of passion changes. Sex is still enjoyable but less thrilling, and less frequent. This is normal. But if sexual contact is drastically reduced, it may be an indication of other problems that need to be solved.

Possibly your girl-friend is falling out of love. Or there could be someone else. She may be angry and resentful, and withholding sex may be her way of showing dissatisfaction. Is sex as good for her as it is for you? Are you a gentle, considerate partner and lover? Do you express your love in non-sexual ways, such as holding hands, cuddling and kissing, without the expectation that it necessarily will end up in the sack?

Talk about your feelings, needs and fears, and encourage her to express hers. Listen—really listen; try to understand and accept her feelings. This takes time and patience, but the situation won't get better all by itself.

Also, you can satisfy yourself sexually by masturbating. This will take the emphasis off sex and put more on the relationship. Good luck.

• ▲ •

How do you overcome your sexual hang-ups?

Sexual hang-ups come to us from our society—family, religion, and peers—in the form of taboos that may or may not be valid. You have to look closely at your attitudes: where did you acquire them and why? Do they reflect reality? Do these values really apply for you? If not, they're hang-ups. You have every right to re-evaluate attitudes and values in light of new information, awareness, and insights.

Talk to your friends, your parents, a counsellor. A good book to read is *Changing Bodies, Changing Lives* (see Bibliography).

It has been said that changing an attitude is about as easy as rearranging a graveyard. This is largely true— by the time we reach adolescence, most of our values and attitudes have been established. But this does not mean that we cannot continue to work on ourselves, and change and grow with experience and knowledge.

• ▲ •

I have a friend who is confined to a wheelchair because

of a spinal-cord injury from a diving accident. Will he ever be able to have sex?

A lot depends on the extent of the injury, its location, and his expectations of what constitutes having sex. Spinal-cord injuries result in varying degrees of disability, and it's impossible to tell from your description the extent of your friend's problem.

The most important point for you to bear in mind is —don't regard your friend as neuter and therefore exclude him from discussions about sex. He's still male, he's still sexually curious, and he's still horny.

As I have tried to point out throughout this book, there are lots of ways to express yourself sexually other than sexual intercourse. As with many other disabilities, people who have had injuries to the spinal cord can be amazingly adaptable and innovative.

• ▲ •

How come girls who fool around are known as sleazes, but guys just get a reputation for being cool?

It's called the double standard, and you're right—it's not fair. Many people used to believe that it's okay for a male to have sex before marriage, but a female should learn about sex only from her husband. This idea stemmed partly from the outdated misconception that "nice girls" don't have sexual thoughts or urges.

Another reason probably has to do with the male ego. Males are still pressured to seem knowledgeable about sex even when they are not, and so may feel inadequate if their girl-friends appear to have more sexual experience than they do.

Personally I feel that "what's sauce for the goose is sauce for the gander." Both males and females have a sex drive; both are capable of starting an unplanned pregnancy, getting and spreading STDs and HIV (AIDS virus). These are good reasons for both sexes to avoid sexual relationships until marriage. Reputation aside, it is just plain stupid for either males or females to "sleep around."

• ▲ •

Are guys hornier than girls?

This is a tough question because everybody's sex drive, or libido, is different. Generally, an adolescent male has the highest sex drive he will ever have. He has frequent spontaneous erections and wet dreams, experiments a lot with masturbation and seems more or less at the mercy of his hormones. By age twenty, things may have settled down a bit: his sex drive is not quite so high, and he feels more in control and comfortable with his sexuality.

Females *appear* to have a lower sex drive as teenagers, but it's hard to say if the reasons are biological or social, since parents and society often convey the mistaken message that "nice girls" aren't interested in sex. But by their early twenties, females start to come into their own. As they become more comfortable with their bodies, they show an increased interest in sex.

Apart from these generalities, neither sex has a monopoly on sexual feelings. People's appetite for sex varies, just as their appetite for food does. Your libido will increase and decrease over your life-time in response to many variables, including age, stress level, fitness, self-image, and the quality of your relationships. The trick is to enjoy where you are right now.

9

The Big "O"

Until recently, people didn't talk much about orgasms. If you had them, that was a great bonus to your sexual relationship; if you did not have them, no one thought anything was wrong. Orgasm was not seen as essential for enjoying sexual activity.

Then in 1966 sex researchers William Masters and Virginia Johnson published *Human Sexual Response*, the result of years of studies and surveys. Although "the Big O" was only one subject touched on by the husband-and-wife team, the media picked up on it. Suddenly, people felt they had to have an orgasm every time they had sex. Simultaneous orgasms (both partners experiencing orgasm at the same time), seemed preferable to separate orgasms. Females were expected to have multiple orgasms. This emphasis on performance put a great deal of pressure on couples. He *had* to be a good lover to bring her to orgasm and she *had* to have an orgasm every time or else she was frigid. For the first time in history, sex seemed in danger of becoming more work than play. This was too bad, and certainly not what Masters and Johnson intended.

Fortunately, we've learned to relax a bit in the years since then. Now we know it's possible to have a wonderful, pleasurable, satisfying sexual relationship *without* necessarily having an orgasm. Some females never achieve orgasm, but still enjoy sex.

Read about it, learn about it, talk about it—but please do not make orgasm the goal of every sexual encounter.

•   ▲   •

What is an orgasm?

Orgasm has been described as the ultimate high of sexual activity. When a male or female becomes very aroused, either with masturbation, heavy petting, oral-genital stimulation or sexual intercourse, the pulse rate and breathing speed up, and tension builds in the muscles throughout the body. With orgasm, there is an explosive feeling of release from this tension. The sensation is most intense in the genitals, although the whole body is involved.

Generally, both partners do not experience orgasm at the same time. While "simultaneous orgasm" sounds passionate and romantic, half the pleasure of sex is enjoying your partner's responses. During your orgasm, you are so preoccupied with your own pleasure that you do not really enjoy your partner's.

When the male ejaculates, he may also experience orgasm. His erection will go down for some minutes or hours, which is known as the refractory phase. During this time, he may continue to stimulate his partner manually or orally, and she may experience one or more (multiple) orgasms.

•   ▲   •

How will I know if I am having an orgasm? When my boy-friend and I get into heavy petting I get these contractions and a tingling, then I get all tense and excited and my legs start to shake. As soon as we have intercourse, it stops. Are we doing something wrong?

You're not doing anything wrong; you're on the way to hitting the peak.

Surprisingly, most women do not experience orgasm during intercourse. Orgasms are triggered by clitoral stimulation, but the clitoris is often not stimulated enough during intercourse. While the repeated thrusting of the penis into the vagina—downward and to the back—may pull the clitoral hood back and forth over the clitoris, this may not be enough to cause orgasm. So don't expect an orgasm from intercourse; it may happen, but is often more likely to occur during heavy petting, oral-genital kissing, licking and sucking in gentle and changing patterns.

You will know you are having an orgasm when the sensations come in waves and the feelings are more intense. Let your body go with it; just *let it happen.* You will experience a high level of sexual excitement, and suddenly POW!—a peak, then relaxation, a slow-down, and a glorious feeling of tranquillity.

• ▲ •

Does orgasm feel different for girls and guys?

Nope—both males and females can register 10 on the Richter scale. But different people experience orgasm in different ways—a "tingling," a "rush," an "explosion" are some of the ways people describe this sensation.

Orgasm feels more intense at different times, and

with different kinds of stimulation. The orgasm you have while masturbating on your own may not be the same as the orgasm you have during intercourse, and different again from an orgasm triggered by oral-genital sex. Amazing!

•   ▲   •

Is it okay to have an orgasm from petting? We have never gone all the way, but whenever my boy-friend and I are into heavy petting I get this wonderful "rush," and then I am wasted.

It is absolutely, perfectly okay. Most females experience their first orgasm by masturbating—alone or with a partner.

My only concern is that, having gone this far with sexual activity, you need to realize that it will not be long before you go all the way. So now is the time to talk with your boy-friend about protecting yourselves from unplanned pregnancy, STDs and HIV (AIDS virus).

•   ▲   •

I have heard that females can have two kinds of orgasms and that one is better than the other. Is this true?

There has been some debate over whether orgasms that resulted from vaginal stimulation by the penis during intercourse were more "mature" or intense than those arising from clitoral stimulation.

We now know that the nerve receptors that trigger female orgasm are mainly centred in the clitoris; the vagina, except for its sensitive outer one-third, contains very few nerve endings. So most orgasms are the result of clitoral stimulation.

It's not important where orgasms come from. It's just nice to have one—though still not essential to enjoying sexual activity.

• ▲ •

What is the G Spot?

Very little is known about the Graffenburg, or "G," Spot; it's not an area you can locate and mark with an X. But the top front wall of the vagina is composed of soft, spongy tissue that is extremely sensitive to sexual stimulation.

If clitoral and vaginal stimulation continue after orgasm, some females experience a tremendous desire to "push," similar to "bearing down" sensations experienced during delivery of a baby. If the female goes with this urge, she may ejaculate a large quantity of fluid from her urethra. This can be embarrassing the first time it happens, because she may think she has accidentally urinated.

Although the fluid spurts from the urethra, it is not urine; it is clear, smells a bit like clover and does not stain the sheets. Researchers believe it results from stimulation of the Skene's glands located around the vaginal opening. In females with very strong pelvic muscles, the fluid may spurt, or "shoot," like a male's ejaculation.

I'd hate to see couples become preoccupied in the search for the "G" Spot. If you accidentally luck into it, great, but it's not essential for sexual satisfaction and pleasure.

•   ▲   •

How come, after sex, the first thing my boy-friend says is, "Did you cum?" He is always upset and disappointed when I answer no, even though I enjoy sex and am not feeling frustrated.

Who has the problem? You're not complaining; you're fine. Your boy-friend is experiencing a sense of failure. In spite of your reassurances, he feels he is not a good lover.

Many males feel they have to "give" their partner an orgasm every time they have sex. If they don't succeed they feel inadequate and may try to shift this inadequacy to their partner, implying that something is wrong with *her*. Your boy-friend needs to recognize that it's unrealistic of him to expect you to have an orgasm every time you have sex.

Continue to let him know that having an orgasm isn't important to you, that you enjoy sex with him, and that he should relax and do the same.

•   ▲   •

Why does it take girls longer to become sexually aroused and to have an orgasm?

It doesn't necessarily take females longer to become aroused. Hugging, kissing and petting can be just as much of a turn on for females as males. A female can be just as horny as her partner but simply because she does not have that obvious indicator (an erect penis) he may not know how turned on she actually is.

Reaching orgasm is another matter. Often it *does* take longer for a female to have an orgasm than it does for a male; she may need more stimulation where she likes it and how she likes it. So take your time and don't rush things.

• ▲ •

I am an eighteen-year-old girl and I go to fitness classes about three times a week. When I do push-ups, sometimes I get an orgasm, and it feels just great. Why does this happen?

This is a great advertisement for staying in shape. A possible explanation: when you exercise, you release hormones called endorphins, which produce a "high" and a sense of power and control over your body.

And since push-ups are pretty boring, your mind may be flipping into a fantasy—perhaps sexual—and this results in a state of arousal. The exercise provides some light clitoral friction, which may trigger an orgasm.

Wonderful—go for the burn!

• ▲ •

Does a guy have an orgasm every time he has sex?

Not necessarily. When a male has intercourse, he will usually shoot or ejaculate, and it will feel good and satisfying. But every once in a while it will be spectacular—wow, boom, bang!

Orgasm is wonderful when it happens, and if it doesn't happen every time, he will still enjoy sex.

• ▲ •

Sometimes when I have sex with a girl I cum within thirty seconds. What can I do?

This is called premature ejaculation and is not unusual. A young, relatively inexperienced male who is very sexually aroused may ejaculate even before his zipper is undone. This is normal and will not necessarily continue in the future.

Here are some of the reasons for premature ejaculation:

Inexperience. You're just not sure of the "moves."

Urgency. You are super turned-on and out of control.

Stress. You're at a party and in a hurry; or you're at her place and her parents may be on their way home; or you're just afraid this may be your only chance.

Fear. "What if she gets pregnant? What if I get the clap, herpes, AIDS . . .?"

Anxiety. "Is my penis too small or too big? Will it fit? Will I hurt her? Am I doing it right? What if she starts to laugh? Will she tell her friends what a jerk I am?"

How can you prevent premature ejaculation? Well . . .

- Avoid "quickie" sex.
- Choose a partner who cares for you, someone

you feel comfortable with and who isn't going to put you down.
- Have condoms ready for protection.
- Try masturbating ahead of time to reduce the urgency.
- Know that if you do cum before you want to, it is not the end of the world. After ejaculation, there will be about a twenty-minute refractory phase when you will lose your erection. Continue stimulating your partner, and by the time you are ready again she will be more aroused than ever.

If you experience premature ejaculation frequently and you are concerned, it helps to become aware of the sensations that precede ejaculation. Try this when you are alone masturbating: just before you think you are about to ejaculate, stop stimulation and allow the erection to subside. Then re-stimulate, and stop again. All this helps you identify the pre-ejaculatory sensations. So when you are with a partner, and you feel these sensations, you'll know when to slow down.

And if your erection does go down, it will come back very quickly, and you'll be off and running again.

• ▲ •

I heard there is a spray that guys can use to keep from cumming too soon. What is it?

I have heard of guys using hair-styling mousse, spray starch, sunburn spray and other stuff to make their erections last longer. Forget it. Other things that won't work include drinking or taking drugs. Don't try to distract yourself during sex by thinking about an up-coming math exam or yesterday's fight with your parents; don't try tensing your muscles, squeezing your buns together, biting your lips or digging your nails into your palms.

A better approach is to talk about your feelings with your partner. That will help you take the emphasis off performance and put it back on pleasure.

There is a wonderful book called *Lasting Longer* by Dr. Sy Silverberg (see Bibliography). I recommend it to anyone who is concerned about premature ejaculation.

•   ▲   •

When I have sex, it takes me a long time to cum, like up to three hours. I have erections and can ejaculate with masturbation and oral-genital sex, but not intercourse.

You have just described a classic case of retarded ejaculation. Somehow, the emphasis in sex for you has shifted from "enjoying" to "cumming," and this expectation has put you under a great deal of stress. You can relax and enjoy masturbation or oral-genital sex because you don't feel any pressure to perform.

You might try to re-evaluate your expectations of sexual activity. Instead of worrying about when and how you ejaculate, enjoy foreplay, including oral-genital sex and mutual masturbation. Have intercourse, but don't expect to ejaculate. If you feel the need to ejaculate, go back to manual or oral-genital stimulation.

This will remove the expectation that you must cum every single time you have intercourse. If it happens, great; if not, that's okay too.

Once you can stop looking at retarded ejaculation as a problem, it will cease to *be* a problem.

• ▲ •

How come I can have an orgasm every time I masturbate but never during sex with my boy-friend. We have tried everything. What could be wrong?

Wonderful question! Sexual intercourse (penis in vagina) may not provide enough clitoral stimulation, so you might ask your partner to spend more time with foreplay—kissing and caressing and just generally building up sexual excitement. And some females find that some positions offer more stimulation that others. Experiment to find which position is best for you.

It's not necessary to have an orgasm in order to enjoy intercourse. Males don't automatically know how to please a female, and since every woman is different, you need to be able to tell him what feels good. Say things like "Ah! I like it when you do that," or gently take his hand in yours to show him what feels best for you.

You can also stimulate your own clitoris with your hand while your partner's penis is thrusting into your vagina. Some males may feel threatened by this at first, but once your partner sees how masturbation increases your mutual pleasure, he may appreciate having the pressure of "giving" you an orgasm taken off him.

Do read the book *For Yourself* by Lonnie Barbach (see Bibliography) for some practical suggestions. And please—don't worry.

• ▲ •

I heard that women who are not able to have an orgasm and who go for sex therapy are taught to masturbate. Is this true?

You heard right. Women who have not yet reached orgasm with a sexual partner are encouraged, even taught, to masturbate in order to find out what pleases them, what feels good, what turns them on. Learning to relax and enjoy one's body makes sex with a partner that much more enjoyable. Once a woman has learned what pleases her, she can teach her partner. The partner can then incorporate this information into his foreplay and bring her to orgasm.

Sex therapists William Masters and Virginia Johnson, a husband-and-wife research team, discovered that most of the women they interviewed had experienced their first orgasm either through solitary masturbation or masturbation with their partner. They also found that orgasms achieved through masturbation are frequently more intense than those experienced during intercourse.

10

Surviving a Break-up

As the song says, "Breaking up is hard to do." Perhaps this Neil Sedaka song is popular because it expresses so well all the loneliness, emptiness and pain we feel at the end of a relationship. Another popular song says, "The first cut is the deepest, baby."

Sooner or later, somewhere along the line, most people experience the sudden break-up of a love relationship. Some cope better than others, but the process is much the same for everybody. Sometimes that process is a little easier if we understand its stages and can give our feelings a name.

Many teens believe the myth that each of us has only one love. This isn't true. To survive a break-up is to learn that you are capable of loving a variety of people for a variety of reasons. You will love again—not immediately, but it *will* happen.

• ▲ •

I want to break up. How should I do it?

Please be honest—if you ever cared for your partner—you have to tell him or her of your "change of heart." You don't have to be brutally honest; you can simply say "My love for you has changed. I don't want to deceive you and I don't want to hurt you—so I think it is only fair to let you know" or "I feel really bad about this but I have met another person and I really find I care for them" or "We are so different—we really have very little in common" or "I am really aware how much we fight and argue and that is destructive behaviour for both of us."

You will notice—*all* of the above involve open, honest, upfront communication.

Please:

- DO NOT dump the person by breaking a date or not returning phone calls. This is painful and not fair.
- DO NOT go out with anybody else "on the sly" until you have separated with your original partner.
- DO NOT spread nasty rumours about your soon-to-be "ex." This only makes *you* look bad.
- DO NOT pick a big fight and storm off without being honest.
- DO NOT ignore the person, be rude or put the person down. This is playing dirty and your "ex" deserves better than that.

If you can't talk about it—write a letter explaining your reasons and feelings. But do it; in the least painful way for both of you.

•   ▲   •

One night, out of the clear blue sky, my boy-friend said he wanted to break up with me. We were so good together. How could he do this to me?

The last two sentences in your letter say so much about the pain, loneliness and confusion people experience in the break-up of a love relationship.

You imply there were no indications that your relationship was in trouble. But somewhere along the line there probably were signs that things were not right—at least, not right for him.

What is clear is that the level of communication between you and your boy-friend was not great. He was unable, or unwilling, to tell you how he was feeling till —suddenly—the situation became intolerable to him. Or, he was giving you messages that you chose to ignore. Either way, he wanted out—leaving you devastated, bewildered and hurt beyond words.

I think it is important that you both sit down and talk about what happened and the feelings you are experiencing—not with the idea of getting back together again, but so you can know what went wrong. Both of you will want to avoid the same problems in future relationships. Also, it is essential to have a sense of finality. It's over. Period.

Think back over your time together. Analyse what happened, so that next time you can recognize and deal with problems as they come up.

· ▲ ·

My girl-friend and I just broke up. I can't stop thinking about her, and it hurts so much I can't believe it.

Yes, it's a lousy feeling. Life has no meaning, and you fell empty, lost and alone. After the initial shock of the break-up, there is the realization that you have to get on with your life, no matter how impossible that may seem.

It's a confusing time. Your feelings may range from mad to glad to sad and back again—all in a matter of minutes or hours.

The mad, or angry, feeling may stem from a sense of being used, manipulated or exploited. The glad feeling may be a sense of relief, of freedom from the hassles and disappointments. But the most common feeling is sadness: we are talking major depression here. You may be so down that you are practically immobilized; you cry, you mope around, unable to think about anything else, such as school, family or friends.

Sounds terminal, doesn't it? But there *is* hope, believe me. You are going through the process of grieving, not unlike mourning the death of a friend or relative, and it takes time. Identifying the stages of this process will help you survive it.

Stage #1: Denial. At first you may think, "This is not really happening to me," "She'll come back to me," or "We can work it out." But soon you'll realize that it *is* happening. And it's over.

Stage #2: Depression. Your sadness is so deep that you may withdraw, even think about suicide. Guys may have a hard time expressing their sadness and loss. This "stiff upper lip" attitude makes those feelings even more difficult and painful. Most females cry on their friends' shoulders, which is great.

Stage #3: Bargaining. You may find that you want your girl-friend back so badly that you will go along with anything just to be together again, such as promising to change some behaviour that your partner finds objectionable, or perhaps having unwanted sexual relations. But this bargaining usually fails.

Stage #4: Anger and revenge. Suddenly all your suppressed resentment bubbles over: "That bitch, I'll show her . . ." or "How could she do this to me, I'll get even with her . . ." While it's normal to have such feelings, it's not appropriate to act on them. At best you'll end up looking dumb. At this stage, you may find yourself getting involved on the rebound in another relationship to prove you are attractive and desirable, or to get even with your "ex." Not good reasons to jump into another relationship.

Stage #5: Acceptance. It's over, finished, that's it, it's done. At last you are free to move on, knowing that sooner or later there will be another significant love in your life.

All this will happen without any help from you. It's just something you have to live through. And you will.

Even after the worst is over, there is the possibility of a relapse. You are sailing along, coping well, and POW! —something triggers a flood of memories and you're zapped all over again. This time it's shorter, not as intense. Soon the relapses become less frequent, until they stop altogether. There's an old adage that time heals all—and it does, believe me.

• ▲ •

How long does it take to get over a break-up?

It depends, often, upon how long you were together,

how close and how intimate you and your partner were. But usually you have to go through all the "seasons": the first snowfall, Christmas, Valentine's Day, summer holidays, all the birthdays and anniversaries you celebrated together. Each special day has its own bittersweet memories, which must be dealt with and put away. By the following year you may still think of that lost love, but it will not be as painful. You may even find that what you miss most is the companionship, rather than that particular person. Now you're ready to be with someone else.

• ▲ •

My boy-friend and I recently broke up. He has a new girl-friend and I'm still miserable.

It's the pits, isn't it? But there are some things you can do to survive this lousy time in your life.

Cry. It's the best way to express your hurt and anger. Or punch a pillow, or fill a plastic bag with scrunched newspapers and kick it around.

Get together with your friends. They understand what you are going through and will listen and be supportive. It's great to talk about your feelings, but use some discretion in discussing your "ex." Resist the temptation to put him down; it only makes *you* look bad.

Keep a diary. Put your feelings in writing. It's therapeutic, and it also forces you to look at yourself and change your behaviour so that you don't make the same mistake all over again.

Meet other guys. It will be difficult at first; you'll
find yourself comparing everyone to your "ex."
It's true no one will ever be quite the same—
probably just as well, because the original was
obviously not right for you.

Get rid of sentimental stuff. All those little
mementoes of happy, loving times—the records,
ticket stubs, stuffed animals—will only make
you sad and slow down the healing process.

Get involved in physical activity. Join a swim
team; check out the Y; go skiing on the
weekends. You'll feel better, and you'll make
new friends.

Talk to your parents. It may seem amazing, but
they know something is going on and they are
concerned. Some of the things they may say
may not be very helpful, but they will
understand and support you.

Take care of yourself. Eat well, but don't pig out.
Get enough sleep, but don't use sleep as an
escape.

Know that you are a survivor. You will come out of
this a winner—stronger, more self-confident and more
aware of what you want from a relationship. So, while
it hurts like hell now, it is a learning, not just a healing,
process. You will survive, grow—and flourish.

• ▲ •

*I've broken up with my boy-friend and I know I'll never
love again. I keep thinking about him and comparing
every other guy to him.*

Obviously, this was a very special relationship. You miss him, and it hurts to know it is over between you.

Getting over the break-up is going to take time, no question about that. The key is to allow the healing to take place. That means:

- Let your sadness go. Don't hang onto it, nurture or cultivate it.
- Don't compare every male to your old boyfriend.
- Be open, receptive and accepting of other people.
- Allow the wonderful, spontaneous you to emerge again and shine.

I know it seems difficult to imagine, but you will meet many other wonderful guys, and one who is just as special as your "ex." And you will love again.

• ▲ •

When a couple breaks up, who seems to suffer most— the girl or the guy?

Both suffer, but a female shows it more than a male. Guys seem able to pick up, brush themselves off and get on with it, while girls become depressed, lonely, introverted, angry, or all four.

Females often seem convinced that they will never love again. Males, on the other hand, tend to establish a new relationship almost immediately, often repeating the same behaviour that caused the break-up of the first relationship.

There are exceptions, of course. And whether you

are male or female, a break-up is probably much easier if you are the "breaker" rather than the "breakee."

• ▲ •

My girl-friend broke up with me last month and I am a disaster. I miss her so much, life has no meaning and I have thought of ending it all.

I wish there was something I could say that would help ease the pain. But that aching, empty void hurts like mad, and nothing I can tell you will change that right now.

My usual advice to people getting over a break-up is to talk to your parents and friends, cry, write your feelings down or record them on tape, keep hyper-busy, socialize. But if you are so depressed that you are feeling suicidal, the very last thing you will be interested in is socializing.

What you do need is somebody you can really talk to. Ask your school nurse of guidance office for a referral to a psychologist or a mental health clinic. You are very upset and distraught; you need and deserve help. Please get it.

• ▲ •

My boy-friend only comes over to my place once a week. That is the only time I see him and he never calls. He says he loves me and we have great sex. But I am wondering if I should break up with him.

When the time is right for you to end it, you will know. Breaking up is inevitable when:

- You feel you have no control over the relationship, and are not getting what you want and need from your partner.
- You sense that your partner does not really care for you.
- You find that you are critical of your boy-friend, angry and resentful even when you're together.
- You get strong messages from your friends or parents that this relationship leaves a lot to be desired. Sometimes outsiders can see things more clearly than the ones who are emotionally involved.

A good question to ask yourself in making this decision is, "Where do I want to be in two years' time?" If things are not getting better, imagine yourself still in the same situation a couple of years down the road, facing the same problems with this guy. Is that what you want?

Tell your boy-friend how you're feeling, and if he is unwilling to spend more time with you, the relationship is doomed. If you decide to make the break, make it clean: over, finished and done with. It won't be easy, but you will feel better in the end. You deserve better.

11

A Baby—Maybe

It is estimated that close to 50 percent of kids do not use effective contraception the first time they have sex. In fact, many continue to have unprotected sex until they have a pregnancy scare.

Panic! Her period is due; it does not come. Frantically, she tries all the folk remedies she has ever heard to bring on her period—castor oil, jogging, jumping off the chesterfield. Nothing works. Finally, she has a pregnancy test at the drug store or her doctor's office.

A negative test result is usually enough to convince most couples to use contraception. But some are not so lucky. They "get caught." The statistics are that one in ten—10 percent—will get pregnant before she graduates from high school. Awesome!

I hope all kids read this chapter. It is not designed to scare you, but to make you aware. Once you understand the fear, sadness and regret both partners feel with a teen pregnancy, hopefully you will decide to abstain from sex for now, or at least obtain a good method of birth control.

How old do you have to be to get pregnant?

It doesn't matter how old you are. If you're menstruating, you probably are ovulating, and if you're ovulating and have unprotected sex, you can get pregnant.

The menstrual cycles of teenagers are often irregular and unpredictable at the beginning. You may have a period, and then not menstruate again for several months. But do not assume that you won't get pregnant just because you are not menstruating regularly. If you do decide to have sex, you *must* use birth control to prevent pregnancy.

• ▲ •

What are the early signs of pregnancy?

The most obvious sign is a missed period. By this time, you may notice other possible indications of pregnancy. These may include:

Fatigue. You are absolutely pooped and want to nap all the time.

Change in eating patterns. You are always starving or you have lost your appetite.

Breast changes. Your breasts may be slightly larger, fuller and tender; the nipples may change from pink to a brownish colour.

Nausea. Although it is called "morning sickness," the urge to barf may occur at any time of the day.

Frequent urination. You feel you've got to pee,

right now; but when you get to the bathroom, there are only a few drops of urine.

Any of these signs can be caused by other things and do not necessarily mean you are pregnant. As well, you could be pregnant and still have a shorter, lighter period (called spotting) for up to three months after conception. So if there is the slightest chance you may be pregnant, have a pregnancy test as soon as possible; do not delay. This can be done at your family doctor's office, a family-planning clinic, or by a pharmacist at a drug store. Do *not* rely on a home pregnancy test kit. Then you will know for sure, and can make some decisions.

• ▲ •

I'm scared I might be pregnant. What should I do?

First, find someone you can talk to—your boy-friend, mother, aunt, sister, or best girl-friend. Then phone your family doctor or family-planning clinic and make an appointment for a pregnancy test as soon as possible. They will do a simple blood or urine test to tell whether you are pregnant.

Or, you make take a urine sample in a clean bottle to your local drug store and ask the pharmacist to do a pregnancy test. This costs about twelve dollars, and you will have the results in two hours. There are home pregnancy-test kits you can buy at the pharmacy, but I don't recommend them—the results are not always accurate.

If you go to your doctor or a clinic, they will also do a pelvic exam to confirm whether or not you are pregnant and determine the approximate stage of the pregnancy.

If you are *not* pregnant, this is a great chance to get a method of birth control, so that you don't go through this panic again.

If you *are* pregnant, then you and your boy-friend have some major decisions to make. You basically have four choices:

- Marry him and keep the baby.
- Stay single, have the baby and raise it on your own.
- Have the baby and put it up for adoption.
- Terminate the pregnancy by a therapeutic abortion.

There are so many things you have to consider. If you marry, your most immediate problem will be finances —how will you and your boy-friend support yourselves and a baby? Will your parents help you out? Will you continue to go to school? Do either of you intend to go to college? If you drop out to care for the baby, what are your prospects for future employment? How mature are you and your boy-friend? Are you both ready to take care of a child, a job that will last for the next twenty years? Is your relationship strong enough to survive? Some teens, particularly those who have physical, emotional and financial help from their families, do go on to become good parents. You have to evaluate your situation—and avoid romanticizing motherhood.

If you choose to be a single mother, you will face many of the same questions—but alone. Being a single mom is rough in terms of finances, affordable day-care, job opportunities, continuing education, possible isolation from family and friends, and future prospects for dating and marriage.

Giving the baby up for adoption is hard, no question about it. But giving it up will be less painful if you realize that you are unable to give the child everything a stable adoptive family can offer.

The decision to have a therapeutic abortion is emotional and difficult. You have to decide how this pregnancy will affect you—and your future.

For a teenager the prospect of an unplanned pregnancy can be terrifying. But ignoring it will not make the problem go away. Think about it. Talk it over with a counsellor, and make the decision that is right for you.

· ▲ ·

I have just found out I am pregnant and I am very confused. Who can I talk to about it?

Your best bet is to look in the blue pages of the phone directory in the Municipalities section. Under "Public Health" you will see phone numbers for Family Planning. Or, make an appointment with your local Planned Parenthood Association—listed in the white pages of the phone book under Planned Parenthood.

Your school nurse could discuss all the alternatives with you. You could also ask your family doctor for information, but if he or she avoids discussing *all* the alternatives, then find another doctor who will.

It is essential that you are offered all the options—including abortion. Be sure you have all the information you want before you make your decision. Because it is *your* decision and nobody should try to influence you one way or another.

· ▲ ·

How can I tell my parents I'm pregnant? I'm afraid they'll kill me.

No, they won't kill you, but they will probably be upset, angry and disappointed. They may also feel a real sense of failure as parents. If you can understand why they are reacting this way, you can avoid a major scene, knowing that in all probability they will come around and support whatever decision you make. Your parents will probably come through in a way that may surprise you.

But if your parents just can't handle it, there are homes for pregnant teens in every city. Consult the Directory at the back of this book or ask your doctor, school nurse, guidance counsellor, minister, Planned Parenthood Association or birth-control clinic for a list of homes in your area.

• ▲ •

When a girl accidently gets pregnant, everyone worries about her. But what about the guy? How does he feel?

Often he's a mess. He is usually terrified—of his parents, her parents, and the prospect of marriage and fatherhood. He may suffer tremendous guilt—"It's my fault. If only I'd worn a condom."

Then there is the feeling of powerlessness. Because although he is as involved as his girl-friend, he has no legal say in her final decision. If she decides to keep the baby, he may wonder what his role should be. Is he ready for marriage and fatherhood? If not, what is his responsibility to her and the child? If she puts the baby up for adoption, he may be jolted by the sudden realization that *his* child will be out there somewhere and he'll never have the chance to know it. If she opts for an abortion, and he feels abortion is morally wrong, again, he has no say in her final decision and may feel guilty, angry and resentful.

It's easy for a guy in this situation to feel abandoned and left out. Hopefully, he can talk to his girl-friend about his feelings, and they can reach a decision together.

• ▲ •

I'm pregnant and have decided to keep my baby. What do I do next?

Take care of yourself.

- Eat a balanced diet. Cut down on junk foods, and drink lots of milk.
- Get plenty of rest.
- Do not smoke, drink alcohol or take any medication not prescribed by your doctor.
- Go to your doctor for regular check-ups.
- Phone your municipal Department of Health for the times and locations of pre-natal classes. Sign up and go!
- Read all you can about pregnancy, labour, delivery, baby and child care.
- Find a group for teen moms in your area.
- Try to continue school and complete your year, if at all possible.

The best of luck to both you and the baby.

• ▲ •

I would like to have my baby and give it up for adoption. How can I do this?

You have two options. You can put the baby up for adoption through the Children's Aid Society. Call them and they will explain the process to you. Or you can speak to your doctor who can help arrange an adoption.

This has probably been a very tough decision for you to make. You deserve all the best.

•　▲　•

I'm pregnant and my parents have kicked me out of the house. Where can I go?

Most communities have homes for unwed mothers. Planned Parenthood or the Children's Aid Society will give you a list of the homes in your area.

•　▲　•

How do you feel about abortion?

I don't like abortion. I don't know anybody who likes abortion. In a perfect world, it would be unnecessary. We would have birth-control methods that were 100 percent effective, and every child would be a wanted child.

But this is not a perfect world. Comprehensive sex education is not taught across the country, so some kids are denied the necessary information. Other kids have the information, but have not developed the decision-making skills to implement it. Finally, no existing method of birth control (except the word "no") is safe, 100 percent effective, inexpensive and easily available.

I work hard to make abortion obsolete. The only way to do this is through continuing research, sex education and easier availability of birth control.

• ▲ •

Do your parents have to be informed if you want an abortion?

In Canada, any female sixteen or older can legally obtain an abortion without parental consent.

If you are under sixteen and your parents refuse consent, you may still be able to get an abortion by having a Legal Aid lawyer obtain "emancipated adolescent" status for you. This may take some time, so don't delay; look in the white pages of the phone directory under "Legal Aid." Abortion is available in the United States to females of any age without parental consent.

If you do not have your parents' approval, it's a good idea to find another adult who will provide emotional support—an older sister, favourite aunt, boy-friend's or girl-friend's mother.

• ▲ •

I know some teens who get pregnant choose to have an abortion? What do the others do?

Teens who have plans for their future—who want to go to college and have a profession before they marry and start a family—are generally the ones who choose to have an abortion. Most of them want to be parents *someday*, but not right now.

Teens who are unhappy at home and do not enjoy school are generally the ones who choose to keep the baby. Often they see having a baby as a way out. They hope a child will provide them with the love they feel they have missed—but they may end up disillusioned when reality sinks in: babies demand more love and attention than they give back. As well, teen parents have poor job prospects, and Mother's Allowance or welfare barely cover necessities.

Although being a single parent is tough, teen moms do well if they have supportive families who will ease the financial strain, help with the baby, offer advice and occasional baby-sitting. Unfortunately, young mothers who do not have such support will find it difficult to be the good, loving parents they want to be.

Some teens decide to continue the pregnancy and put the baby up for adoption.

I don't believe that anyone facing an unplanned pregnancy should base her decision on what anybody else chooses to do. You have to do what's best for you.

• ▲ •

How is an abortion done?

The easiest, cheapest, fastest and safest procedure is a D&E, or dilatation and evacuation. While some doctors will consider doing a D&E up to the sixteenth week of pregnancy, most doctors in Canada will not consider performing a D&E after twelve to fourteen weeks. So if you choose to have an abortion, you haven't got much time to make a decision. There are a few variations of the D&E, but the process is basically the same for all of them. Under either a local or general anaesthetic, the cervix is dilated (expanded), and the endometrial lining of the uterus along with the embryo is removed.

After the operation, a counsellor discusses birth control with the patient, and after a snack and a rest, she may go home.

Because the cervix may take up to three weeks to close again, the female must avoid tub baths (showers are okay), swimming, tampons and intercourse during this time to reduce the risk of infection. There will be some bleeding for ten days to three weeks; the blood will be bright red a first, then turn dark brown and taper off. If she develops a fever, begins to bleed heavily or pass blood clots, she must go to the emergency department of the nearest hospital immediately.

Abortion is a simple surgical procedure, but there are risks involved. Do not consider having one performed by anyone except a doctor in a recognized hospital or clinic.

Most females feel an intense sense of relief after the surgery and are determined that it will never happen again.

• ▲ •

What is salting out?

This is a slang term for a type of abortion that may be performed if the female is sixteen to twenty-four weeks, or four to six months pregnant. She is admitted to hospital, and an ultrasound test will be done to confirm the stage of pregnancy. A saline solution (salt water) is injected into the amniotic sac, which contains the fetus in the uterus. This induces labour, and the embryo is delivered. It will not be born alive.

This is a traumatic procedure, emotionally as well as physically. The patient must stay in hospital for three days or more. The cost is covered by your provincial health plan.

An abortion is much easier and safer if it is performed before the twelfth week of pregnancy. So please, if there is the least possibility you may be pregnant, have a pregnancy test as soon as possible—then make your decision. Should you choose abortion, you have to act on your decision immediately.

If you do require a saline abortion, don't try to get through it alone. You need the love and support of your partner, your family and your friends.

•   ▲   •

What do you have to do to get an abortion?

Getting an abortion is *not* easy. Many doctors and hospitals refuse to perform the surgery, and in some communities, abortion is not available. So don't think that if you get pregnant abortion would be an easy answer. Avoid complicating your life by always using effective birth control.

Once your pregnancy has been confirmed by a doctor, if you decide to have an abortion, you will be referred either to a clinic or to a specialist (obstetrician-gynaecologist) who will perform the surgery in a hospital. In some localities the abortion may safely be done by a local doctor who is specially trained.

Some Canadian women who cannot obtain an abortion in their own community choose to go to an abortion clinic in the United States.

• ▲ •

If a girl has an abortion, will it be more difficult or impossible for her to become pregnant in the future?

No. An abortion performed by a doctor is quite safe. Still, it must not be considered a method of birth control. Three or more abortions may result in "cervical incompetence," which means the female may have trouble carrying a pregnancy to full term in the future.

• ▲ •

One of my girl-friends had an abortion and was just fine, but now I've had one and I've been a basket case these last couple of months.

It's impossible to predict how different people will react, emotionally, to an abortion. Most females are initially relieved that it's all over. There is sometimes even a feeling of euphoria. But after a few days, you may find yourself with a real case of the blues. This is normal, the result of the hormones swinging back to the pre-pregnant state. It will take a few weeks for your regular cycle to re-establish itself. If you find yourself crying for no reason at all, or just feeling blah, it's okay —these feelings are valid; you have just suffered a loss and are grieving. But if the depression does not lift or lasts longer than a month, go back to your doctor.

Then there are the "anniversary blues." One year after the abortion, you may suddenly think: "A year ago I had an abortion. The baby would be about six months old right now. I wonder if it was a boy or a girl. . . . I wonder what it looked like. . . ."

At this point, it's time to go over your reasons for having an abortion. I call it self-talk, and it goes like this: "If I'd had the baby, where would I be right now? Would I have had to quit school? Would I have a scuzzy job? Would I have been able to look after the baby? Would my boy-friend and family have hung in there with me?"

The important thing here is to realize that sometimes things happen that we wish had not happened. But no one is born mature; maturity comes only through experience. When we make mistakes, we can try to put them to good use by learning not to repeat them.

Even after you've passed this hurdle, it's not unusual to have another setback a few years later. By then, you will have got your life in order and be functioning well. Then suddenly, POW!—you will see someone with a beautiful baby, and you'll think, "Isn't he gorgeous— the same age mine would have been if only . . ." At this point you will stop, and go through the same self-talk as you did the first time.

Years later when you are cuddling your own planned, wanted, and loved baby, you may think, "I ended a life just like this one—how could I have done it?" Painful. Again, back to square one for some self-talk: "If I'd had that first baby, would I have this one now? Would I have my present partner? Would my family have been as delighted with that baby as they are

with this one? Would I have been as secure financially
and emotionally as I am now, ready and able to be a
good parent?"

So you see, the emotional fall-out from an abortion
may last for years. If you experience chronic depression, go back to the doctor or clinic that performed the
abortion and talk about it. They can refer you to a
counsellor who will help you deal with your feelings.

• ▲ •

*Right after the abortion they put me on the birth-
control pill, even though I swore I was never going to
have sex again. Why?*

It's understandable that, after an abortion, the idea of
sex is enough to turn you off. But there are medical
reasons you may be prescribed the birth-control pills:

- The pill will regulate your menstrual cycle so
  that you will have a period three weeks after
  surgery and every twenty-eight days after that as
  long as you are on the pill.
- It makes the uterus contract, stopping post-
  operative bleeding.
- It will prevent a repeat pregnancy just in case
  you change your mind and have sex.

It's a good idea to stay on the pill for about three
months after an abortion. By then, you will have sorted
out your feelings and decided what you want in life. If
at this point you are not sexually active, it's okay to go
off the pill, but be certain to use a good method of birth
control if you do resume having sex.

If you prefer not to go on the pill, say so and discuss other methods of birth control with the counsellor. Just be sure you have a good method of birth control should you decide to have sex.

• ▲ •

My boy-friend and I broke up three months after I got pregnant. Could the pregnancy have caused the break-up?

It may have helped. An unplanned pregnancy does place phenomenal stress on a teenage relationship. With all that fear, anxiety, guilt and anger, it's amazing when a relationship does survive. The prospect of parenthood is frightening. He could not handle the stress and pressure, and so opted out; you *had* to cope, with or without him.

And you made it. So don't dwell on your bad feelings, but get on with your life. Probably you won't settle for less than a good, committed relationship in the future.

• ▲ •

After my mother found out I had an abortion, her whole attitude toward me changed—she began treating me like an adult, and we were much closer. But my father would not speak to me or even look at me for weeks. How come?

I am constantly amazed at the number of kids who say they actually become closer to their parents after telling them they were—or are—pregnant. It's a helluva way to get close to your folks, but it seems to work.

There are many reasons that may account for *your* mother's reaction. She may be impressed with the way you handled the situation—you made the decisions, the appointments, and went through it on your own. Now she views you as an adult. Or, the experience may have triggered some memories for your mother. If the same thing once happened to her, she may empathize with you.

Your father's reaction reveals his disappointment that you did not live up to his idealized image of you. It may be difficult for him to accept that his "little girl" is a sexually active adult. Give him time; when his hurt heals, he will realize that you are human, and worthy of his trust and love.

• ▲ •

I used to be dead-set against abortion, but now that I'm pregnant I know it's the only solution for me. But I still don't feel right about it.

You sound like a sensitive, aware young lady. I am impressed that you have been able to make and accept such a difficult decision.

This was not something you foresaw in your life-script, and it's tough to have to re-think your values. You have examined the alternatives, and you know what's best for you at this time, but that doesn't make it any easier. It's difficult, and it hurts.

12

The Care & Feeding of Parents

Most parents have a very difficult time talking to their kids about sex. Sex is so personal, so private, intimate. Parents are reluctant to admit that they do not know everything there is to know about sex and sexuality. And some parents are convinced that the minute they talk about sex they are giving kids permission to "do it." But research has proven that just because kids know about sex, it doesn't mean that they're going to do it the first chance they get.

The concern parents feel has not changed from generation to generation. The fear of sexually transmitted diseases has now been compounded by the terror of AIDS. An unplanned pregnancy is another valid worry. Your parents are also concerned that you will get a "bad reputation." So they are trying to protect you. They also don't want you to be hurt emotionally.

Believe me—they have your best interests at heart— but when it comes to sex parents seem to lose their normal cool.

In this chapter I explore some of the ways you can approach your parents on the difficult topic of sex. Try them—you'll be amazed.

Do my parents still do it?

I hope so. Kids have a hard time imagining mom and dad having a grand and glorious sexual romp.

We need to acknowledge that everyone—even your parents—is a sexual being. From the time we are born, everything we say and do expresses our sexuality. This is normal, natural and wonderful.

Just because your parents have been married and have had kids does not mean that they have lost interest in sex.

You know those Saturday mornings when your folks lock the bedroom door, saying they want to sleep in? Well, guess what they're *really* doing.

• ▲ •

My mother read my diary and found out that my boy-friend and I had been petting. She freaked out! How can I get her to stop snooping around my stuff?

All kids are entitled to space of their own and some privacy. But some parents rummage through their kids' purses, read their mail, open their diaries, listen in on telephone conversations. Without excusing such behaviour, I think it might help to understand why your mother does this. She probably feels that something is going on between you and your boy-friend. She's terrified that you'll get pregnant or get a disease, but she doesn't know how to talk to you. Reading your diary is one way to find out just what you're up to.

Sit down and quietly tell your mom that you need to write all your feelings and experiences in your own diary without fear that anyone else but you will read it. Or you could write only dull, boring stuff for a few months—then mom will decide nothing is going on. But I hope your mother will agree to respect your right to privacy. That is the best way to make sure the lines of communication between you stay open.

As for the petting, most mothers are not delighted when they discover their daughter is fooling around. Mom's concerns are valid. Are you protecting yourself by practising safer sex? If you are, gently reassure her you are being careful. If you are not practising safer sex, your mother has a right to be worried. Get the protection you may need and let her know you'll use it.

• ▲ •

I'd like to ask my parents about sex, but don't know how.

It is much easier to talk to your parents if you have been asking questions right along. If you wait until you have a real problem your folks will probably go into shock.

Start out by asking simple, easy questions. Once you get an answer, be sure to say, "Thanks, Mom—now I know where to go for information." This relaxes and reassures mom so that she feels better about "talking sex" with you.

There are other safe openers:

- "Mom—the kids were saying. . . . Is that true?"
- "Dad—is it normal for a guy . . .?"
- "This article in the newspaper on AIDS says. . . ."
- "We had this class in school and someone mentioned French kissing. What is that?"
- "I have to do a project on abortion. How do you feel about it?"

- "One of the Grade 12 girls is pregnant. Boy—that scares me."
- "Dad—there is this guy at school and the kids say he's gay. What does that mean?"
- "Mom—how do you feel about people living together before they are married?"

Or you could leave this book on the coffee-table. That ought to start something.

• ▲ •

My parents found a copy of my dad's skin magazine under my mattress and they were just furious. Why is it okay for dad and not for me?

Fantastic question. I understand why you resent their reaction, but you need to understand how your parents feel. They may be concerned that learning about sex from a skin magazine might give you the wrong idea, or encourage you to become sexually active before you are ready to handle it emotionally. As for dad, he probably feels that as a grown-up he is better able to keep sex in its proper perspective.

My concern with sexually explicit magazines is their heavy emphasis on the performance aspect of sex—penis size, getting it up, keeping it up, keeping score. They seldom give information about birth control, STDs or HIV (AIDS virus), nor do they talk about love, caring, commitment and communication. They also encourage unrealistic expectations about our partners, since few of us have bodies like the centrefolds of *Playboy* and *Playgirl*. But there are some pluses: these magazines are stimulating, make us more aware that we are sexual beings, and sort of give us permission to fantasize—and that's great.

Sit down with your parents, ask them what their objections are and listen carefully to their response. Then tell them your feelings. Maybe you can come to an understanding. If they see that you are responsible in your attitudes about sex, they will realize that your reading these magazines now and again is not the end of the world.

• ▲ •

How come I can talk about anything with my boy-friend's mother, but not with my own?

This kind of thing is not unusual. Your boy-friend's mother can afford to be relaxed, casual and accepting with you because you are not *her* child. If you were, she'd be more critical, more judgmental and more anxious for you to develop the right attitudes and behaviour. In other words, she would act pretty much the way your mother probably does.

A well-known child psychologist, Dr. Lee Salk, says that we are all great parents to everybody's kids but our own. Maybe if everyone exchanged kids every six months, we'd all be fine.

You're lucky your boy-friend's mother is so approachable. Be sure you let her know you appreciate her.

• ▲ •

My girl-friend and I come from different ethnic and religious backgrounds. Her family doesn't seem to accept me no matter what I do and won't let me see her.

Wow, you've hit a double-whammy here. Many people hold prejudices against those who come from a different racial, religious or cultural background. Although these opinions usually have no rational basis, they are difficult to counter because people rarely admit to having them.

It would be easier for your girl-friend to try to talk to her parents about why they disapprove of you. Perhaps then she can reassure them that it is possible for people of different cultures and religions to be together. You need to know that she may not be able to convince them, but at least she tried.

If this doesn't work, you and your girl-friend have to make some difficult choices.

- You can continue your relationship in secret until you are old enough to make a commitment. While it is possible that her parents may feel differently in a few years' time, this course of action is risky. If they find out, they will cease to trust their daughter and may blame you for "leading her astray."
- You can defy her parents by continuing your relationship openly. You won't have to deal with guilt about sneaking around behind their backs, but her parents will probably try everything to keep you apart—threats, grounding, cutting off her allowance. Life will not be easy—for her, or for you.
- If your relationship is strong enough to survive the wait, you can decide to cool it for now and reassess the situation in a couple of years' time.
- You can decide that, in spite of your feelings for each other, this relationship is doomed, and agree to break up.

This is really being caught between a rock and a hard place. Good luck—you're going to need it.

• ▲ •

My dad and I used to be a lot closer than we are now. He used to hug me, but not anymore.

I hear this from teens, both male and female. As you go through puberty and your body develops, your parents suddenly become self-conscious about physical contact with you. It's too bad, because we all need to be touched and hugged.

It is difficult for parents to acknowledge that their kids are sexual beings. Dad may be convinced that feeling attracted to his lovely daughter is abnormal, and rather than acknowledge those feelings he simply avoids physical contact. His daughter—not understanding what is going on—may misinterpret this as rejection. Father may also pull away from his son for fear that touching will be interpreted as a homosexual overture, or that he might make his son gay. Mother may have difficulty accepting her attraction to her gorgeous son.

But feeling attracted to someone in your family does not mean you are on the verge of incest. It's okay to be attracted—these feelings are normal, natural and harmless. In misunderstanding them, we miss out on a lot of warmth and affection.

• ▲ •

I just can't figure out what's going on with my mom. One minute she's laughing and joking, the next minute she's crying her eyes out.

If you think it's tough for you, think how tough it must be for your mother. My guess is that your mother is going through menopause, or the "change of life." This usually happens between the ages of forty-five and fifty-five, when the ovaries stop producing the female hormones estrogen and progesterone. Menstruation becomes irregular and gradually ceases; ovulation also gradually stops. Menopause may trigger other physical and psychological changes. Your mother may experience "hot flashes," unpleasant and sudden sensations of heat travelling through the body, sometimes with profuse sweating. She may have mood swings such as you describe; she may not sleep well at night and be irritable the next day.

Another serious, long-term side effect of menopause is a loss of calcium from the bones. Later this may result in osteoporosis: bones break easily, heal slowly, the spinal column shrinks, and some women may lose one or two inches in height. Females of all ages can reduce the risk of osteoporosis by drinking a quart of milk a day, or eating other dairy products such as cheese and yoghurt.

Menopause may take its toll on mom's self-image and self-esteem. The best thing your mother can do right now is take extra-good care of herself; a balanced diet and a moderate exercise program will help her handle the stress of menopause and keep her feeling fit. If her symptoms are severe, her doctor may prescribe hormone-replacement therapy.

You can help a lot by being understanding, loving and supportive, and sparing her unnecessary hassles. Think of it this way: mom saw you through diapers, chicken pox, braces and acne. Now is your chance to reciprocate.

• ▲ •

Will my dad go through the "change of life" too?

Male "menopause" is less obvious, but middle age may be trying for dad too. After about age fifty his testosterone (male sex hormone) level drops, and he may experience a decrease in sex drive and difficulty having or maintaining an erection. He may become depressed at the realization that he will never become president of his company, or that his children will soon be leaving the family home and will not need him any more.

At this difficult time, your father needs reassurance that he is successful, capable and loved. You can help by understanding what's going on and being supportive.

• ▲ •

My parents are driving me insane. Last week when I came in they were both waiting up for me. Boy, did they ever lace into me. I was late, they don't like my boy-friend, my marks are down, my room is a mess, I spend too much time on the phone, and I didn't take the garbage out. I can't do anything right and I just want to run away.

Sounds like you and your parents have been "gunnysacking"—storing up angry feelings over a period of time rather than expressing them. When you were late, they were worried; then they were relieved you were okay, but furious that you put them through all that anxiety. That, combined with the other accumulated annoyances, triggered the explosion.

You all need some cooling down time. Agree that you'll discuss the situation the next day. Meanwhile, you, mom and dad should each make up a list of your grievances.

Before you and your parents begin the discussion, everyone must acknowledge that the reactions on both sides are valid, and need to be heard and understood. One way to ensure this is to guarantee each person five minutes of speaking time—no interruptions or interrogations. Then take turns, explaining exactly how you feel and why, and how you would prefer things to be. Deal with the most difficult problem first, and stick to the following ground rules for fair fighting:

- No put-downs, insults or sarcasm.
- Do not assign blame ("It's your fault because . . .").
- Do not try to analyse each other ("You're crazy," "You just want to manipulate me . . .").
- Use "I messages" ("When you do this . . . it makes me feel . . .").
- Avoid dragging up the past ("You always . . ."). Concentrate on what's happening now.
- Avoid hearsay evidence ("Jim said that you said . . .").
- Do not threaten. Statements like ". . . or else I'll run away" are manipulative.
- Try to solve one issue at a time.
- Do not call in reinforcements by involving other family members. This is your problem and you must solve it.

Once you've all had your say, outline a contract that is acceptable to everyone. This will require compromise: "Okay, I'd like to stay out till eleven o'clock on school nights, but I realize you feel that is too late. I'll agree to ten o'clock if I can stay out an hour later on the weekends." Agree on appropriate penalties if the contract is broken: "If you are late, you will be grounded Friday night." No punishment should last longer than twenty-four hours.

If you have more than two or three problems to discuss, you'll probably need to have several meetings before they are all settled. All this takes time and determination, but having peace in the family is worth it.

13

On Being Gay

In every school, one in ten males will be gay, and about one in twenty females will be lesbian. With such a high presence it is difficult to understand why our curriculum avoids any discussion of homosexuality and lesbianism. It's no wonder I get so many questions from kids on same-sex relationships.

By age eighteen, most gay and lesbian teens are pretty well aware of their sexual orientation, although it may take them years to be able to accept it, talk about it, or act on it. They may spend a lot of time trying to prove to themselves and others that they are "straight," sometimes having meaningless sexual experiences in order to do so.

The major concern teens have about their homosexuality is that family and friends will reject them. There have also been incidents of "gay bashing" at some schools. Kids' fears of rejection and prejudice are valid, since the issue of homosexuality remains clouded by misinformation and misunderstanding.

Your sexuality is just one of the many facets of your personality. Cultivate your uniqueness, celebrate it—it is what makes you an individual. It is the *real you*.

How do gays and lesbians "do it"?

Sexual expression between males includes kissing, necking, petting and mutual masturbation, oral-genital and anal sex. Lesbians express their sexual feelings in much the same way.

Gay and lesbian sex can be just as loving, tender and meaningful as heterosexual sex may be.

•　▲　•

What causes a guy to be turned on by other guys?

No one knows for sure what causes homosexuality any more than we know what causes heterosexuality. Over the years there have been many theories about what factors make people gay: weak father, dominant mother; dominant father, weak mother; too many hormones; too few hormones. We now know that none of these theories is correct.

Sexual orientation is not a conscious decision; rather, it is a realization. Some researchers suggest that homosexual preferences may be established by age three. By age seven these kids sense they are different; by age nine they know it. By age twelve they must start to deal with their sexuality, and by age eighteen they generally acknowledge that they are homosexual, if only to themselves.

The problem with talking about the causes of homosexuality is that it implies there may be a cure for it. But attempts to change homosexuals into heterosexuals through different kinds of therapy have failed. In fact, most gays and lesbians do not want to be "cured" of their sexual orientation any more than heterosexuals do. Like everyone, they want the three big A's: Approval, Acceptance and Appreciation.

•　▲　•

Aren't same-sex relationships against nature? Animals aren't queer. And if men do not mate with women the race will die out.

Wow—haven't you ever seen one male dog humping another male dog in the park? Monkeys are notorious for same-sex activity, and I once saw two young cows making out in a field. Same-sex behaviour is natural among mammals.

The human race is certainly not endangered from under-population. Over-population, yes; also pollution and the threat of nuclear war. In any case, only about ten percent of the population is homosexual, and most heterosexuals reproduce.

I wonder how you feel about heterosexual couples who make a conscious decision not to have children? Are *they* going against nature?

Biases against people who are different from you— be it race, colour, religion, culture or sexual expression —develop at a very early age. We need to question these strong negative reactions in the light of factual information, then decide if our attitudes are valid. I hope, as you read this chapter, you will gain some new insight into homosexuality and become more tolerant and accepting.

•　▲　•

I am okay with all aspects of homosexuality except that I just can't stand it when they kiss and hug in public. Why do they do this?

Generally for the same reasons that heterosexuals kiss and hug. Casual, public displays of affection are the norm among modern heterosexual couples, so there is no reason gays and lesbians should feel any different about holding hands, hugging or kissing.

Many of us are uncomfortable with overt public displays of sexuality, whether heterosexual or homosexual. You might also react negatively toward a female who wore inappropriately sexy clothing or too much make-up, or to a heterosexual couple engaged in passionate kissing on a bus.

The important thing is to be aware of your reaction and understand it.

• ▲ •

I am not gay, but I went into a bar and this guy tried to make a move on me. Why?

This can and does happen, and heterosexual males get very upset when it does. They wonder if they look gay, or have somehow done something to create the mistaken impression that they were looking for gay sex.

It's nothing to get upset about. Many females are approached by males all the time to have sex, and most learn not to get upset if some jerk makes a move on them. They simply say, "Sorry, no thank you," and move away.

• ▲ •

Why are guys so uncomfortable around gay men? Women don't seem to be too bothered by gay men or lesbians.

We do not know all the causes of homophobia—fear and hatred of homosexuality—but it does seem to develop very early in boys. I suspect their discomfort is based on misconceptions about what a male should be like. Any male who does not conform to the stereotype is in danger of being labeled a "fag."

Females, on the other hand, seem to be more tolerant of homosexuality. At least they are less likely to brand a lesbian as "butch" or a "lezzie."

Some straight males may feel threatened because many females enjoy the company and companionship of gay males, or they may be concerned that they have homosexual tendencies themselves. In denying this, they reject all homosexuals.

One in ten kids is gay. It's sad to think that we make it so difficult for them to be comfortable with their sexual orientation.

• ▲ •

How do you know if you are homosexual or not? I think I may be, and it scares me.

This is a very common concern for kids. We all search for our sexual identity during adolescence. And since many kids engage in some homosexual play when they are very young, or occasionally have same-sex fantasies —all of which are very normal—they sometimes become convinced they are homosexual.

There is always the possibility that you may be gay. Some of the indications are:

- You are not interested in anyone of the opposite sex, but are attracted to those of the same sex.
- Your sexual fantasies and day-dreams are predominantly of same-sex encounters.
- You sense or know you are different.

Be aware that you may be going through a time in your life when homosexuality holds a particular fascination for you. This does not necessarily mean that you are homosexual. Also, you don't have to decide whether you are or not by midnight tonight. If you are, it will become clear in a few years, and if not you will know that, too.

But this is a tough thing to deal with on your own, and if it is really bothering you, then the best thing is to seek counselling or contact one of the gay youth support groups listed in the directory at the back of this book.

• ▲ •

I am eighteen years old and gay. I would like to be able to tell my parents, but I don't know how.

Acknowledging your homosexuality is known as coming out. Coming out to your parents is probably the biggest and hardest step you will ever take, because the fear of rejection is so strong. After all, we spend most of our lives trying to win our parents' approval.

Now that you've decided to tell them, choose the right time. You know your parents, their reactions, and all the factors that will affect the way they accept your news. If your younger brother has just totalled the car, now is not a great time to say, "Oh, by the way, folks—I'm gay."

Anticipate your parents' reactions. Even if their views on sex are liberal, it's unlikely they will stand up and cheer on learning their child is gay. Most parents expect their kids to marry and present them with grandchildren, and you have now all but eliminated this hope. There may be tears, anger—"How could you do this to us?"—or denial—"Don't worry, it's just a phase you're going through." In any case, they will need time to get used to the idea. Remember, you have had months or years to come to terms with your sexuality, so don't pressure them for instant acceptance. You or your parents might write to an organization called Parents of Gays (see the Directory at the back of this book); its members provide counselling and support.

Whatever their initial reaction, most parents come around in time and accept their child's homosexuality. In fact, many know or suspect when a son or daughter is gay or lesbian, but do not know how to broach the subject. So discussing it openly is often a relief for everyone.

Before you raise the subject with your parents, you need to know that you can and will survive with or without their acceptance of your homosexuality.

• ▲ •

I think I may be a lesbian. I have never been interested in guys at all, and am very attracted to a friend at school who I know is a lesbian. We talk, but I am scared to go farther than that.

What are you afraid will happen if you open up and

discuss your feelings with your friend? If she is a lesbian as you say, she will not be offended; on the contrary, she may be flattered. So what is the worst thing that can happen?

Well, she might not be interested in you romantically; she may have a steady girl-friend, or is getting over a relationship and needs time on her own. In any case, she will tell you. You may be disappointed, but it will not kill you; and knowing for sure is better than the uncertainty and anxiety you are putting yourself through now.

And you don't have to pledge undying love right off the bat. You might begin by telling her about your experiences dating guys, and how you did not enjoy it; you could tell her you are lonely, enjoy having her for friend and would really like to get closer to her. You may also want to contact a gay and lesbian youth group where you can get support and learn more about the "coming out" process.

•　▲　•

I am gay and lonely. Where can I go to meet gays my own age?

Most large cities have a support system of organized activities for kids who are, or think they may be, homosexual. A phone call to any gay support group is the easiest way of getting a referral (or see the Directory at the back of this book). But for high school kids who do not live in big urban areas, life can be difficult and very lonely.

There are probably a few other kids around who feel the same sense of isolation because of their sexual orientation. But you may want to be discreet and keep a low profile. Many kids play it straight until they finish school; life tends to get easier after that. So hang in there.

•   ▲   •

I am gay and I hate it. I want to be like everybody else and marry and have kids. Please give me the name of a therapist who will make me heterosexual.

You are obviously having a difficult time with your sexual orientation, and yes, I would like you to have some counselling for what appears to be a major issue in your life. But no qualified therapist would try to make you heterosexual—that would not work, and the experience could be traumatic. What a therapist *would* do is to help you focus on your negative feelings and put them into perspective, so that you can be more comfortable with your homosexuality.

If having kids is a major concern, please know that there are areas in the United States where gay males can adopt and raise children. Perhaps this will one day be the case in Canada. I know some lesbians who have had children by a male friend, and actively involve him in child raising. So that, too, is a possibility.

Phone or write to a gay support group in your area (see the Directory at the back of this book). Ask for a list of "gay positive" counsellors and make an appointment with one to discuss your feelings.

And good luck. This is a tough one to work out, but you can emerge stronger and more positive if you are willing to face it.

•   ▲   •

Do all homosexuals cruise?

Not all homosexuals cruise—that is, make the rounds of gay bars specifically looking for casual sexual contacts. On the contrary, many homosexuals are involved in long-term, stable, committed, loving relationships. Gays who cruise do so not because they are homosexual, but because of an individual need. Many straight males cruise heterosexual bars for the same reason. In this age of AIDS, cruising is high-risk behaviour. To put it bluntly, it's just plain dumb—for heterosexuals and homosexuals.

• ▲ •

My mother separated from my dad after twenty years of marriage because she is a lesbian. Does this mean I will be a lesbian too?

No. There is no evidence that children of homosexuals show a higher incidence of homosexuality than children of heterosexuals. We do know that if there is one homosexual child in the family, there is a slightly increased probability that there will be more than one. But we have no explanations or theories of why this happens.

By the way, being gay or lesbian does not interfere with being a good parent.

• ▲ •

I get more touching and hugging from a gay male friend than I do from my boy-friend.

I often hear this from females. We all need touching from the time we are born—it is warm, comforting and comfortable, and reassures us that we are accepted and appreciated.

Female infants are often cuddled and held more than males; by adolescence, males have generally learned that the only touching that is appropriate to the male is sexual contact. When a female touches him—holds his hand or strokes his arm—he may misinterpret this as permission to proceed to hugging, petting, and eventually sex. Females pick up on this, and if they don't feel like sex, may back off from hand-holding or hugging. Males interpret this as rejection and stop doing it.

But with a gay friend, sex never enters into it. You both know that there is no danger of misinterpreting a casual hug or kiss as a sexual come-on.

• ▲ •

Do homosexuals get sexually transmitted diseases?

Gay males who are sexually active are susceptible to all STDs. Practising anal sex without a condom is an *extremely* high-risk behaviour and leaves gay males vulnerable to the HIV (AIDS virus). Lesbians can get herpes, crabs, monilia and trichomoniasis from sexual contact with another woman; chlamydia occurs less often, but it's possible. Genital warts, gonorrhea and HIV (AIDS virus) are less common among lesbians than among gay males—unless these women have occasional sexual contact with a straight or bisexual male or female.

Bacteria aren't fussy as long as their surroundings are

dark, wet and warm—which the genitals are. That makes everybody—straights and gays—vulnerable to STDs.

●　▲　●

Do all lesbians use vibrators?

No. Straight males seem to have the idea that lesbians must use a vibrator or dildo (penis-shaped sex toys) as a substitute for the penis, but this is not true. A vibrator may be used for arousal and stimulation, but seldom to simulate intercourse. Heterosexual males and females may also use vibrators this way.

●　▲　●

My boy-friend is bisexual. He says that although he loves me, he also wants to continue seeing a close male friend and occasionally have sex with him. I'm having trouble coping with this.

My initial reaction is one of concern. If your boy-friend is having sex with another male, he is at risk of contracting HIV (AIDS virus); then he could unknowingly infect you with the virus. This is how most women currently get AIDS. If you have not been practising safer sex right from the start of your sexual relationship, it would be a good idea for both of you to be tested for exposure to HIV.

Apart from the health risks involved, it's understandable that you are having trouble coping with this relationship. It is truly an either/or situation: *either* he stops having any sexual contact with any other male, *or* it's over between you.

We have to be realistic here: the chances of him going straight for life are remote. Even if he says he will change, can you ever really trust him? Not only are you going to get hurt, you are risking your life. It's not worth it. Sorry to be so blunt, but it is called reality therapy.

You'll be much better off without him. There are so many other wonderful guys. You'll find one who loves you—who wants you and only you.

• ▲ •

Why do some guys like to wear women's clothes? Does that mean they're gay?

Men who like to wear women's clothes are called transvestites. They are not homosexuals. Most transvestites are heterosexual males; many are married with children. They are usually well-adjusted in other areas of their lives. They may enjoy putting on women's clothes and makeup to go to a bar frequented by other transvestites, or they may simply remain at home, fantasize and perhaps masturbate.

Transvestitism is regarded as harmless. Problems may arise, however, if the transvestite's partner does not understand and accept his behaviour. In most cases, therapy for both partners is necessary if the relationship is in jeopardy.

Drag queens are *not* transvestites. They are homosexual males who often "feel" female and love dressing up in glamorous female clothing and makeup. They are usually more flamboyant than transvestites and enjoy flaunting it.

• ▲ •

What is the difference between a transsexual and a transvestite?

Good question—the words sound similar, but their meanings are very different. While transvestites obtain sexual gratification from wearing women's clothes, transsexuals have the anatomy and physiology of one sex, but passionately believe that they should have been born as the opposite sex. The medical name for transsexualism is gender dysphoria.

Transsexualism affects three times as many males as females. It is *not* the same as homosexuality. A transsexual male may desire a male partner because he sees himself as a female trapped in a male body; a male homosexual simply prefers having a partner of the same sex.

Diagnosis is made after a lengthy psychiatric assessment. A transsexual who wishes a sex-change operation must live and dress as the opposite sex for two years prior to surgery. During this time, a male begins taking female sex hormones to increase his breast size, raise his voice and reduce facial hair. Then, in extensive genital surgery, erectile tissue is removed from the penis and the remaining skin is turned inside out to fashion a vagina. The testicles are transformed into labia. Nerves are transplanted to make a clitoris. The new genitals will provide sexual arousal and satisfaction, but because this new "woman" has no uterus or ovaries, she will not be able to get pregnant.

Transforming a female transsexual into a male is more difficult. She will require breast-reduction surgery as well as genital surgery to close the vaginal vault, fashion a scrotal sac from the labia, and implant silicon testes. Hormone therapy enlarges the clitoris to a size of about two inches, but it will not become large or stiff enough for penetration and intercourse. Alternatively, a female may have a penile implant—a flexible plastic rod that will permit penetration and intercourse.

Because the silicone testes will never produce seminal fluid nor sperm, the new "man" will not be able to father a child.

14

The Scary Side of Sex

I would love to be able to omit this chapter, which deals with the "down" side of sex. Kids hear about it; some are unfortunate enough to experience it.

The statistics are shocking. One out of four females is sexually exploited by a member of her own family. Such sexual abuse (called incest) is especially traumatic because the victim is usually a child who feels powerless to say "no."

Unfortunately, many children who run away from home to escape sexual or other abuse find themselves alone in a big city, working the streets as prostitutes, trapped in the very situation they sought to escape.

We would rather not hear about such things, but they can and do happen. If we know the facts and the effects, we will be better able to deal with them.

• ▲ •

Is sexual assault the same thing as rape?

Sexual assault used to be called rape and was restricted to forced sexual intercourse. The definition has now been broadened into three categories:

Sexual assault. Forced kissing, fondling of your body, particularly the genitals, or sexual intercourse where there is no sign of injury or physical abuse.

Sexual assault with a weapon. Same as above, but the attacker threatens you or a third person with bodily harm with a weapon.

Aggravated sexual assault. A sexual assault during which you are beaten up, or wounded, or in danger of being killed.

Anyone who commits sexual assault can be arrested and prosecuted, and if convicted may serve a jail term.

• ▲ •

Is it true that a girl cannot be raped unless she secretly wants to be raped?

This is a myth. Unfortunately women in our society are not usually brought up to assert themselves, and so may not know how to head off a threatening situation before it becomes dangerous and if it does become dangerous most women have not been trained to defend themselves. And most rapists use threats or physical violence to get what they want. A female may be terrorized into submitting, but this does not mean she consents or wants to be raped.

Here are some other common myths about rape:

Myth. Most rapes are committed by strangers. In more than half of all rapes the attacker is known to the victim—he may be a friend, neighbour, casual date or steady boy-friend—even a husband.

Myth. Rapists are motivated by uncontrollable sexual desire. Rape is an act of violence. The attacker wants to exert dominance and control, and does so by overpowering, humiliating and degrading his victim. He is not necessarily sexually aroused.

Myth. Females get raped only when they pick up guys in bars or wear seductive clothing. While these are dangerous situations, many sexual assaults by strangers occur in or around the female's home—such as the underground parking garage or laundry room.

Myth. Only young, attractive women get raped. Anyone can be sexually assaulted, regardless of age, sex, physical appearance, or life-style.

• ▲ •

My girl-friend was raped one night while walking home from baby-sitting at about nine at night. A man grabbed her from behind, put his hand over her mouth and dragged her into some bushes. Now she is scared to tell her parents, scared to go out, and she cries all the time. She talks to me and I listen, but I don't know what to tell her.

She is lucky to have a good friend like you. Please keep on talking to her, because it may take some time for her to get over this experience. It will be easier for her if you can encourage her to:

Tell her parents. Parents can be very helpful in getting her the medical attention and giving her the emotional support she needs.

Go to her doctor for a check-up, tests for STDs and perhaps a pregnancy test. If she is not comfortable with a male doctor, help her find a supportive female doctor.

Inform the police. Rapists need to be reported, found and charged to protect other females.

Go to the local rape crisis centre and request a referral to a counsellor to help her deal with her feelings. (See the Directory at the back of this book).

You can also reassure her that it was not her fault—no one asks for it just by walking home alone at night. And don't underestimate the value of listening—you are invaluable to her right now, just by being a warm and understanding friend.

• ▲ •

One night my boy-friend and I were necking but I told him over and over I didn't want to go any further. He said I was a tease, got violent, and forced me to have sex. I thought I loved him, but now I'm not sure.

This is called "date rape." I can certainly understand how your feelings toward your boy-friend have changed. You cared for him and believed that he cared for you; you trusted him and he betrayed that trust.

Unfortunately, some males believe they have the right to take what they want. They also believe that because they are sexually aroused, they must have immediate relief. But guys know that they will not die from an erection; they can masturbate if they wish. A male can take care of himself without making some female feel responsible for his sexual gratification.

What your boy-friend did was wrong and was a criminal offence. You have the option of reporting him to the police and pressing charges for sexual assault. It's important for you to realize that you are not to blame for what happened. Your boyfriend had no right to force you into sexual activity you did not want. Right now you need some help. You are probably reluctant to tell your parents. For sure they will be upset and angry at your boyfriend, and maybe angry at you for ever going out with him. But generally, parents understand and can be wonderfully supportive.

You should see a doctor for a check-up to rule out the possibility of pregnancy and STDs. Your doctor can also suggest a counsellor to help you sort out your thoughts and feelings about the assault, your relationship with your boy-friend and your feelings about your own sexuality.

As for your boy-friend, he is bad news; dump him. Let's face it. He is selfish and violent. You do not want either quality in a partner. If he really loved and cared for you he would not threaten and hurt you this way. You deserve a nice guy who loves you, respects you and treats you decently.

• ▲ •

I am a nineteen-year-old guy. Six months ago I was raped by two other guys. They even made me have an erection. I am terrified I might have AIDS, and now I wonder if I'm gay.

Yes—you have really had a traumatic experience, and all your reactions are understandable. Male rape is more common than most people think. Because males are reluctant to talk about it, we often don't hear about male rape. You should phone your local AIDS committee to discuss the possibility of having a test for HIV (AIDS virus). Or ask your family doctor.

Rest assured—forced sexual activity will not make you gay. Heterosexuality or homosexuality is usually established long before a person is seventeen. As for your lack of interest in sex with a female, this is natural under the circumstances. Many people react to sexual assault by denying their sexuality. They may avoid all forms of touching and find sex abhorrent. A good therapist can help you to work through these feelings and come to terms with your experience.

You need to rediscover that you are an okay person with a great deal to offer, and that mutually shared sex can be joyous. Please phone your local rape crisis centre for a referral to a qualified, experienced therapist.

•　▲　•

Is there a right way to defend yourself if you are sexually attacked?

There is no single best way; it depends on the circumstances. Are there people within earshot? Is it possible for you to escape danger by running away? You have to assess the situation at the time fast, and act accordingly.

Most rape crisis centres advise the following as the best tactics:

Scream. If there are people around, they may come to you assistance, or at least call the police. Your screams may scare your attacker off.

Run. This may not help much if you are on a lonely stretch of highway, but if running will get you out of danger, or even buy you some time, by all means do it. Get to a lighted street, a shop, a telephone booth; bang on somebody's door.

Be prepared. The best way to learn effective self-defence is to take a course specifically geared to women, such a Wen-Do. Even if you are never attacked, such training will teach you to think defensively, will give you a sense of self-confidence, and of being in control. It will also help you realize that you are physically stronger than you think you are.

• ▲ •

My boy-friend says he loves me, but he sometimes punches me when he is upset about other things. What can I do?

In simple words—*"Get out of the relationship now."* This jerk is using you as his personal punching bag. It will not get better; it will almost certainly get worse, and you may end up battered or even dead. Avoid having any contact with him at all—no phone calls, no letters, no meetings to patch things up. Do not consider taking him back even if he promises to change: "I miss you, I love you, it won't happen again...." The only way to make sure it will not happen again is to get him out of your life.

But your boyfriend needs help. You could suggest he see a counsellor or therapist.

• ▲ •

When I was thirteen, my stepfather came on to me, and this went on for three years. I told my mother at the time, but she didn't believe me. I have now learned to avoid him, but I am terrified for my younger sister. She is too young to understand and would be too scared to do anything.

Sexual abuse by a family member—a blood relative or otherwise—is called incest. Recent statistics reveal that one in four females is coerced or manipulated into sexual activity by an older member of the family, and the resulting trauma may last for years.

I, too, am very concerned for you and your sister. I think it is essential that you tell somebody. Since your mother did not believe you, consider going to your school nurse, guidance counsellor, family doctor, minister, or a social worker at the Children's Aid Society or check the section on Sexual Abuse in the Directory at the back of this book. All these people are trained to help in such circumstances. They will believe you, they are discreet and will help you avoid repeated abuse and protect your sister.

Incest is a *very* serious problem and it requires intervention by experienced counsellors. You could also join an "incest survivors" therapy group to help you understand that you are not to blame for what happened. You did not ask for it, nor did you deserve it. Counselling or therapy will provide you with the opportunity to work through your feelings of anger and resentment, shame and regret, distrust and fear. The transition from "victim" to "survivor" to "winner" is much easier when you have counselling.

I am impressed with your concern and desire to protect your younger sister. Now—for your sake as well as hers—get the help and support you need.

• ▲ •

When I was fourteen my uncle began touching me sexually, and this went on for about a year and a half. I have read that incest is supposed to be devastating, but for me it wasn't. Sometimes I even enjoyed it, and still use some of these experiences in my sexual fantasies. Is this abnormal?

No, it is not abnormal, though it is unusual. Sexual abuse affects different people in different ways. While many females react to incest by rejecting sex entirely, others do not necessarily feel that they were used, manipulated or coerced into sexual activity.

There are many possible explanations of why the experience was less traumatic for you. Could it be that you did not feel manipulated or controlled by your uncle? You may have been flattered by the attention, needed the affection, or felt this was a safe way to satisfy your curiosity about sex.

Just because the experience was not negative for you does not alter the fact that what your uncle did was wrong and illegal. He misused his position of authority and trust within the family.

As for your reactions—there is no such thing as abnormal. Don't let anybody tell you how *you* should feel. You got through a potentially traumatic situation and came out a winner.

• ▲ •

I was walking home from school when this man came toward me with his raincoat open and his thing in his hand. I crossed the street and went into a store till he went away. What should I have done?

You did exactly what you should have done. What this man was doing is called exhibitionism, and males who do it get their jollies from your reactions. It would have been sexually stimulating for him had you panicked and screamed, or run away crying. By avoiding him, you prevented him from getting much satisfaction, and he left.

Once you were safely in the store, it would have been a good idea to report this incident to the police.

Also called flashers, exhibitionists are generally harmless, but their sexual behaviour is unacceptable in society and can be upsetting to others—especially to children.

• ▲ •

What is S&M? And what is bondage?

S&M is a slang term for sado-masochism. "Sado" refers to sadist, someone who becomes sexually aroused by inflicting pain on another. A masochist, on the other hand, is someone who enjoys receiving pain—being spanked, whipped, or generally forced into painful sexual practices.

Bondage means tying up, perhaps even gagging and beating your sexual partner, with or without his or her consent.

These practices can be dangerous, because in the heat of passion, you can get carried away and cause injury to your partner or yourself. Personally, I feel S&M and bondage are best left in the realm of fantasy.

• ▲ •

Why do guys go to prostitutes?

Prostitution is sometimes called the world's oldest profession. Before Christianity, prostitutes worked in the local temple and paid its bills with their earnings.

There are many reasons for going to a prostitute (also called hooker, whore, street-walker, call-girl, lady-of-the-evening, working girl). Young males may go to lose their virginity, hoping to learn about sex from a pro; older males may be looking for variety and excitement, or simply unemotional, uninvolved, uncommitted sex where there is no obligation to go through romantic rituals or foreplay. Others may visit a prostitute to relieve sexual tension when their regular partner is absent, ill or unwilling to engage in sex or they have no regular partner and want *some*one. A person who uses the services of a prostitute is called a john or a trick.

There are male prostitutes, as well. Some serve females as paid companions and sexual partners; others sell oral-genital or anal sex to other males.

Personally, prostitution does not upset me, as long as the prostitute is over eighteen and independent of a pimp—a person, usually a male, who lines up clients and protects her, yet who often abuses his "girl-friend" while living off her earnings. Some European cities have legalized prostitution and have ensured that prostitutes get regular medical check-ups; but some people regard this as legalizing sin, and so disapprove.

• ▲ •

I am fifteen. Two years ago I ran away from home because I was fighting with my parents constantly. To make a long story short, I ended up working the streets. I have had gonorrhea three times and my pimp sometimes beats me up. I have to get out of this, but I can't go home. What can I do?

The first step is to get out of danger and off the streets —which amounts to the same thing. Find a youth hostel or safe house where you can eat and sleep, get counselling, a job referral or help returning to school. Please see the Directory at the back of this book.

I am concerned about your personal safety with your pimp. You may think he loves you—but he doesn't. He's a pimp, that's all. Once you have figured out where you can go, *leave*—do not give him any warning, or try to go back for your clothes, or reveal your whereabouts to friends who could tell him. If he does find you and threatens you in any way, report him to the police.

Your safe house will help you get family counselling

should you change your mind about going home. Give it some thought—it does work sometimes.

This is one of the hardest situations to get out of, so make use of all available support services. And don't give up. Once you've made the decision to get out, you are well on your way.

There are many questions that I have not been able to include. I have the feeling we have only scratched the surface.

But I hope that this book is a step toward information and understanding, and that as questions arise, you will be able to talk to your parents, an older sister or brother, an aunt or uncle, good friend or a special teacher.

My ultimate goal is not just to give information about sex, but to make you aware of yourself as a sexual human being with the self-confidence to make informed decisions about sex—including your right to say "no."

Sex can be wonderful if it is what you want, when you want it, with the person you want, and provided you have taken precautions to prevent pregnancy, sexually transmitted diseases, and HIV (AIDS virus).

This is a tall order for a teenager, but please do not settle for less.

Because you are worth it.

Directory: Where to Go for Help

This directory lists some of the places you can go for help or more information. We were not able to include all the clinics and counselling centres across Canada, so check your local phone book for additional listings.

Clinics for birth control counselling, pregnancy tests, diagnosis and treatment of STDs

For all regions, phone the Public Health Department listed in the blue pages of your phone book.

ALBERTA

Women's Health Centre
Grace Hospital, 1402—8 Avenue, Calgary, Alta. T2N 1B9
(403) 284-1141, EXT. 394

Edmonton Board of Health Birth Control Clinic
10010—105 Street, Edmonton, Alta. T5J 1C8
(403) 425-5850

BRITISH COLUMBIA

East Vancouver Youth Clinic
2610 Victoria Drive, Vancouver, B.C. V5N 4L2
(604) 872-2511

Knight Youth Clinic
6405 Knight Street, Vancouver, B.C. V5P 2V9
(604) 321-6151

Main Street Youth Clinic
3998 Main Street, Vancouver, B.C.
(604) 261-6366

Pine Clinic
1985 West 4 Avenue, Vancouver, B.C.
(604) 736-2391

Vancouver Women's Health Collective
302—1720 Grant Street, Vancouver, B.C.
(604) 255-8285

MANITOBA

Manitoba Health & Community Services
Brandon: (204) 728-7000
Beauséjour: (204) 268-1411
Dauphin: (204) 638-8785
Flin Flon: (204) 687-3457
Portage la Prairie: (204) 857-9711
Selkirk: (204) 482-4511
The Pas: (204) 623-6411
Thompson: (204) 778-7371

Health Action Centre
425 Elgin Avenue, Winnipeg, Man.
(204) 947-1626

Klinic
545 Broadway Avenue, Winnipeg, Man. R3C 0W3
(204) 786-6978

Mount Carmel Clinic
886 Main Street, Winnipeg, Man.
(204) 582-2311

Women's Health Teen Clinic
304—414 Graham Avenue, Winnipeg, Man. R3C 0L8
(204) 947-1517

NEW BRUNSWICK

Victoria Health Centre
65 Brunswick Street, Fredericton, N.B. E3B 1B5
(506) 453-2136

NEWFOUNDLAND & LABRADOR

Planned Parenthood Newfoundland/Labrador
203 Merrymeeting Road, St. John's, Nfld. A1C 2W6
(709) 579-1009

NOVA SCOTIA

Cumberland County Family Planning Association
16 Church Street, Amherst, N.S. B4H 4B8
(902) 455-9656

NORTHWEST TERRITORIES

Contact your local Nursing Station or Public Health Centre
for information and referral.

ONTARIO

Bay Centre for Birth Control
901 Bay Street, Toronto, Ont. M5S 1Z7
(416) 323-6010

Birth Control & VD Information Centre
2828 Bathurst Street, Suite 501, Toronto, Ont. M5B 3A7
(416) 789-4541

Crossways Clinic
2340 Dundas Street West, Toronto, Ont.
(416) 534-2041

Hospital for Sick Children Adolescent Clinic
555 University Avenue, Toronto, Ont.
(416) 598-5804

Hassle Free Clinic
556 Church Street, Toronto, Ont. M4Y 2E3
(416) 922-0566 (females)
(416) 922-0603 (males)

South Riverdale Clinic
126 Pape Avenue, Toronto, Ont.
(416) 461-2493

Women's College Hospital Youth Clinic
76 Grenville, Toronto, Ont.
(416) 323-6061

Serena Toronto
252 Newton Drive, Toronto, Ont.
(416) 221-9962

PRINCE EDWARD ISLAND

Public Health Nursing Office
Charlottetown: (902) 892-1001
Summerside: (902) 436-9124

QUEBEC

Centre régional de planification familiale
1814 rue Deschênes, Jonquière, P.Q. G7S 4K6
(418) 548-4785

Centre de santé des femmes de Montréal
16 boulevard St-Joseph est, Montreal, P.Q. H2T 1G8
(514) 842-8903

SASKATCHEWAN

Department of Public Health
Regina: (306) 522-3621
Saskatoon: (306) 664-9626

YUKON

Department of Health and Human Resources
(403) 667-5474

General information about birth control, sexually transmitted diseases and pregnancy counselling.

For all regions, phone your local Planned Parenthood Association listed in your phone book.

ALBERTA

Calgary Birth Control Association
223—12 Avenue S.W., Calgary, Alta. T2R 0G9
(403) 261-9821

MANITOBA

Facts of Life Line
(204) 947-9222
Outside Winnipeg but within Manitoba 1-800-432-1957

NEW BRUNSWICK

Reproductive Health Clinic
55 Lobban Avenue, Chatham, N.B. E1N 3A8
(506) 773-9887

Reproductive Health Clinic
100 Arden Street, Suite 603, Moncton, N.B. E1C 4B7
(506) 857-5999

NOVA SCOTIA

Women's Health Education Network
P.O.B. 999, Debert, N.S. B0M 1G0
(902) 662-2424

Women's Health & Medicine Committee
Box 400, Sir Charles Tupper Medical Building, Dalhousie University,
Halifax, N.S. B3H 4H7
(902) 425-4514

Picton County Women's Centre
P.O.B. 964, New Glasgow, N.S.
(902) 755-4647

Family Planning Resource Team
P.O.B. 1598, Sydney, N.S. B1P 6R8
(902) 539-5158

ONTARIO

STD (Sexually Transmitted Disease)
Information Line
392-7400

Women's Health Interaction
58 Arthur Street, Ottawa, Ont. K1R 7B9
(613) 563-4801

PRINCE EDWARD ISLAND

Teen Health Information Line
(902) 368-4357

QUEBEC

Service d'information en contraception et sexualité de Québec
797 chemin Ste-Foy, 3rd Floor, Québec, P.Q. G1S 2K5
(418) 681-2181

SASKATCHEWAN

Regina Healthsharing
P.O.B. 734, Regina, Sask. S4P 3A8
(306) 352-1540

AIDS Committees

ALBERTA

AIDS Calgary
223—12 Avenue S.W., Calgary, Alta. T2R 0G9
(403) 262-6446

AIDS Network of Edmonton
Ross Armstrong Office, 10233—98 Street, Edmonton, Alta. T5J 0M7
(403) 429-AIDS

BRITISH COLUMBIA

AIDS Vancouver
Suite 509, 1033 Babie Street, Vancouver, B.C. V6E 1M7
(604) 687-2437

Vancouver PWA Coalition
1170 Bute Street, Vancouver, B.C.
(604) 683-3381

AIDS Vancouver Island
P.O.B. 845, Stn. E., Victoria, B.C. V8W 2R9
(604) 384-4554

MANITOBA

AIDS Advocacy Group
(204) 453-2483

NEW BRUNSWICK

AIDS New Brunswick
Victoria Health Centre, 65 Brunswick Street, Fredericton, N.B.
E3B 1B5
(506) 479-7518

NEWFOUNDLAND & LABRADOR

Newfoundland & Labrador AIDS Association
P.O.B. 1364, Stn. C, St. John's, Nfld. A1C 5N5
(709) 739-7975

NOVA SCOTIA

Metro Area Committee on AIDS
P.O.B. 1013, Stn. M, Halifax, N.S. B3J 2X1

ONTARIO

Hamilton AIDS Network for Dialogue & Support
P.O.B. 146, Stn. A, Hamilton, Ont. L8N 3A2

AIDS Committee of Cambridge, Kitchener, Waterloo & Area
P.O.B. 1925, Stn. C, Kitchener, Ont. N2G 4R4

AIDS Committee of London
649 Colborne Street, London, Ont. N6A 3Z2
(519) 434-8160

AIDS Committee of Ottawa
P.O.B. 3390, Stn. D, Ottawa, Ont. K1P 6H8
(613) 238-1717

AIDS Committee of Regional Niagara
P.O.B. 61, St. Catharines, Ont. L2R 6R4

AIDS Committee of Thunder Bay
19 Regent Street, Thunder Bay, Ont. P7A 5G5
(807) 345-1516

AIDS Committee of Toronto
(mailing address)
P.O.B. 55, Stn. F, Toronto, Ont. M4Y 1G2
(street address)
464 Yonge Street, 2nd floor, Toronto, Ont. M4Y 1W9
(416) 926-0063

AIDS Hotline
(416) 392-AIDS

AIDS Committee of Windsor
P.O.B. 7002, Windsor, Ont. N9C 3Y6

QUEBEC

L'Association des ressources Montréalaises sur le SIDA/Montreal AIDS Resource Committee
1650 boulevard de Maisonneuve ouest, Suite 604, Montreal, P.Q.
H3G 2P3
(514) 937-7596

SASKATCHEWAN

AIDS Regina
P.O.B. 3414, Regina, Sask. S4P 3J8
(306) 522-4522

AIDS Saskatoon
P.O.B. 4062, Saskatoon, Sask. S7K 4E3

Gay and Lesbian Associations

ALBERTA

Gay Youth Calgary
#317 223—12 Avenue S.W., Calgary, Alta. T2R 0G9
(403) 234-8973

Lesbian Information Line
#314 223—12 Avenue S.W., Calgary, Alta. T2R 0G9
(403) 265-9458

Gay/Lesbian Youth Group of Edmonton
P.O.B. 1852, Edmonton, Alta. T5J 2P2
(403) 424-8361

BRITISH COLUMBIA

Vancouver Gay/Lesbian Youth Group
1170 Bute Street, Vancouver, B.C. V6E 1Z6
(604) 684-6869

Island Gay Society—Victoria
P.O.B. 695, Stn. E., Victoria, B.C. V8W 2Y2
(604) 383-9124

MANITOBA

Winnipeg Gay/Lesbian Youth
Box 1142, Winnipeg, Man. R3C 2Y4

NEW BRUNSWICK

Fredericton Lesbians & Gays
P.O.B. 1556, Stn. A, Fredericton, N.B. E3B 5G2
(506) 457-2156

Gais et Lesbiennes de Moncton
P.O.B. 7102, Riverview, N.B. E1B 1V0
(506) 858-1013

NEWFOUNDLAND

Gay Association of Newfoundland
P.O.B. 1364, Stn. C, St. John's, Nfld. A1C 5N5
(709) 739-7975

NOVA SCOTIA

Gay Alliance for Equality
P.O.B. 3611, South Postal Stn., Halifax, N.S. B3J 3K6
(902) 454-6551

ONTARIO

The Gayline
c/o Pink Triangle Services, P.O.B. 3043, Stn. D, Ottawa, Ont.
K1P 6J6
(613) 238-1717

Lesbian & Gay Youth of Toronto
519 Church Street, Toronto, Ont.
(416) 591-6749

Parents & Friends of Lesbians and Gays (Parents FLAG)
35 Willis Drive, Brampton, Ont. L6W 1B2
(416) 457-4570

Parents FLAG
52 Essex Street, Goderich, Ont. N7A 2H4
(519) 524-4879

Parents FLAG
48 Garfield Avenue, London, Ont. N6C 2B5
(519) 432-4581

Toronto Counselling Centre for Lesbians and Gays
105 Carlton Street
Toronto, Ont. M5B 1M2

QUEBEC

Gay Montreal Association/Association homophile de Montréal
P.O.B. 487, Stn. H, Montreal, P.Q. H3G 2L5
(514) 933-2395

SASKATCHEWAN

Gay Information Services of Regina
P.O.B. 3414, Regina, Sask. S4P 3J8
(306) 522-4522

Lesbian Association of Southern Saskatchewan
P.O.B. 4033, Regina, Sask. S4P 3R9
(306) 352-8397

Gay & Lesbian Support Services
P.O.B. 8581, Saskatoon, Sask. S7K 6K7
(306) 665-9129

Sexual Assault/Sexual Abuse/Incest

ALBERTA

Calgary Sexual Assault Centre
1725—12 Street, Calgary, Alta. T2T 3N1
(403) 244-1353

Sexual Assault Centre of Edmonton
#204 10179—105 Street, Edmonton, Alta. T5J 1E2
(403) 423-4121

Lethbridge Sexual Assault Centre
#5 505-7—7 Street South, Lethbridge, Alta. T1J 2G8
(403) 320-7730

BRITISH COLUMBIA

Cowichan Rape/Sexual Assault Centre
P.O.B. 89, Duncan, B.C. V9L 3X1
(604) 748-7273

Fort St. John Rape & Sexual Abuse Centre
10247—100 Avenue, Fort St. John, B.C. V1J 1V8
(604) 785-8811

Kamloops Sexual Assault Counselling Centre
387—4 Avenue, Kamloops, B.C. V2C 3P1
(604) 374-9600

Mid-Island Sexual Assault Centre
101—285 Prideaux, Nanaimo, B.C. V9R 2N2
(604) 753-0022

Sexual Assault Recovery Anonymous
P.O.B. 16, Surrey, B.C. V3T 4W3
(604) 591-9111

Sexual Assault Helpline
#2—3238 Kalum Street, Terrace, B.C. V8G 2N4
(604) 635-4042

Vancouver Rape Relief & Women's Shelter
77—20 Avenue East, Vancouver, B.C. V5V 1L7
(604) 872-8212

Women Against Violence Against Women
204—636 West Broadway, Vancouver, B.C. V5V 1G2
(604) 875-6011

Victoria Women's Sexual Assault Centre
1045 Linden Avenue, Victoria, B.C. V8V 4H3
(604) 385-5545

MANITOBA

YWCA Rape Crisis Service
198—11 Street, Brandon, Man. R7A 4J4
(204) 727-5014

Flin Flon Rape Crisis Centre
130 Green Street, Flin Flon, Man. R8A 0P9
(204) 687-8255

Thompson Rape Crisis Centre
1-55 Selkirk Avenue, Thompson, Man. R8N 0M5
(204) 778-7273

Klinic Sexual Assault Crisis Program
545 Broadway Avenue, Winnipeg, Man. R3C 0W3
(204) 774-4525

NEW BRUNSWICK

Fredericton Rape Crisis Centre
P.O.B. 174, Fredericton, N.B. E3B 4Y9
(506) 454-0437

NEWFOUNDLAND & LABRADOR

Rape Information Centre
c/o Newfoundland Status of Women Council, P.O.B. 6072, St. John's, Nfld.
(709) 726-1411

Happy Valley Rape Crisis Committee
P.O.B. 783, Stn. B., Labrador A0P 1E0
(709) 896-8483

NOVA SCOTIA

Service for Sexual Assault Victims
6450 Young Street, Halifax, N.S. B3L 2A3
(902) 425-0211

ONTARIO

Guelph-Wellington Women in Crisis
P.O.B. 1451, Guelph, Ont. N1H 6N9
(519) 836-5710

Hamilton Rape Crisis Centre
14 Queen Street North, Hamilton, Ont. L8R 2T8
(416) 525-4573

Sexual Assault Centre London
388 Dundas Street, London, Ont. N6B 1V7
(519) 438-2272

Kingston Sexual Assault Crisis Centre
P.O.B. 1461, Kingston, Ont. K7L 5C7
(613) 544-6424

Niagara Region Sexual Assault Centre
5017 Victoria Avenue, Niagara Falls, Ont. L2E 4C9
(416) 356-9662

North Bay Rape Crisis Centre
P.O.B. 1012, North Bay, Ont. P1B 8K3
(705) 476-3355

Sexual Assault Support Centre
P.O.B. 4441, Stn. E, Ottawa, Ont. K1S 5B4
(613) 234-2266

Peterborough Rape Crisis Centre
P.O.B. 1697, Peterborough, Ont. K9J 7S4
(705) 876-9111

Support for Sexual Assault Victims
P.O.B. 2646, Sarnia, Ont.
(519) 337-3320

Barbra Schlifer Commemorative Clinic
188 Dupont St., Toronto, Ont.
(416) 964-3855

Toronto Rape Crisis Centre
P.O.B. 6597, Stn. A, Toronto, Ont. M5W 1X4
(416) 597-1171

Sexual Assault Care Centre
Women's College Hospital
76 Grenville, Toronto, Ont.
(416) 323-6040

Thunder Bay Physical & Sexual Assault Crisis Centre
18—214 Red River Road, Thunder Bay, Ont. P7B 1A6
(807) 344-4502

Windsor Sexual Assault Crisis Centre
14 Hanna Street East, Windsor, Ont. N8X 2M8
(519) 253-9667

PRINCE EDWARD ISLAND

PEI Rape & Sexual Assault Crisis Centre
P.O.B. 1522, Charlottetown, P.E.I. C1A 7N3
(902) 566-8999

QUEBEC

Maison ISA
P.O.B. 1032, Chicoutimi, P.Q. G7H 5G4
(418) 545-6444

Centre d'aide et de lutte contre les agressions à caractère sexuel
P.O.B. 1872, Stn. B, Hull, P.Q. J8X 3Z1
(819) 771-6233

Mouvement contre le viol
P.O.B. 364, Stn. NDG, Montreal, P.Q. H4A 3P7
(514) 842-5040

Centre d'aide et de prévention contre les agressions à caractère sexuel
P.O.B. 1274, Rouyn, P.Q. J9X 6E4
(819) 762-8443

Assaut sexuel secours
P.O.B. 697, Val d'Or, P.Q. J9P 1P6
(819) 824-3572

Centre d'aide et de prévention des assauts sexuels de Valleyfield
P.O.B. 295, Valleyfield, P.Q. J6S 4V6
(514) 371-0145

SASKATCHEWAN

Battleford & Area Sexual Assault Centre
P.O.B. 1044, North Battleford, Sask. S9A 3K2
(306) 446-4444

North East Crisis Intervention Centre
P.O.B. 2066, Melfor, Sask. S0E 1A0
(306) 752-9455

Abortion Clinics

MANITOBA

Morgentaler Clinic
883 Corydon Avenue
Winnipeg, Man.
R3M 0W7
(204) 964-2437

ONTARIO

Morgentaler Clinic
85 Harbord Street, Toronto, Ont.
(416) 964-1174

Scott Clinic
157 Gerrard Street East, Toronto, Ont.
(416) 962-4108

QUEBEC

Morgentaler Clinic
2990 Honoré-Beaugrande, Montreal, P.Q. H1L 5Y6
(514) 351-2522

Abortion Referral

NOVA SCOTIA

**Canadian Abortion Rights Action League/Association canadienne pour le droit
à l'avortement**
P.O.B. 101, Stn. M, Halifax, N.S. B3H 2L4
(902) 422-4123

Crisis shelter and counselling for kids who want to get off the street

ONTARIO

Covenant House
70 Gerrard Street East, Toronto, Ont.
(416) 593-4849

Inner City Youth Program
(counselling only)
151 Gerrard Street East, Toronto, Ont.
(416) 922-3335

Roberston House (females)
291-295 Sherbourne Street, Toronto, Ont.
(416) 392-5650

Mercury Youth Services
385 Yonge Street, Suite 201, Toronto, Ont.
(416) 591-9000

Seaton House (males)
339 George Street, Toronto, Ont.
(416) 392-5522

Street Haven (females)
87 Pembroke Street, Toronto, Ont.
(416) 967-6060

Street Outreach Services
(counselling only)
27 Carlton Street, Suite 408, Toronto, Ont.
(416) 593-4418

Stop 86 (females)
86 Madison Avenue, Toronto, Ont.
(416) 922-3271

YMCA **House** (males)
485 Queen Street West, Toronto, Ont.
(416) 865-9700

Youth Without Shelter
6 Warrendale Court, Rexdale, Ont.
(416) 748-0110

MANITOBA

Baldwin House (females)
860 Preston Avenue, Winnipeg, Man.
(204) 783-7129

SASKATCHEWAN

Rainbow Youth Centre
1806 Albert Street, Regina, Sask.
(306) 757-9743
(306) 525-9779

BIBLIOGRAPHY

Adams, Caren, et al. *No Is Not Enough: Helping Teenagers Avoid Sexual Assault*. San Luis Obispo, CA: Impact Publishers, 1984.

Barbach, Lonnie Garfield. *For Yourself: The Fulfillment of Female Sexuality*. New York: Signet, 1975.

Bell, Ruth, et al. *Changing Bodies, Changing Lives*. New York: Random House, 1980.

Bell, Ruth, et al. *Talking With Your Teenagers: A Book for Parents*. New York: Random House, 1985.

Boston Women's Health Collective. *The New Our Bodies, Ourselves*. New York: Random House, 1980.

Carrera, Dr. Michael. *Sex: The Facts, the Acts and Your Feelings*. New York: Crown Publishers, 1981.

Comfort, Dr. Alex and Jane Comfort. *The Facts of Love: Living, Loving and Growing Up*. New York: Ballentine Books, 1979.

Fraser, Sylvia. *My Father's House: A Memoir of Incest and of Healing*. Toronto: Doubleday, 1987.

Heron, Ann, ed. *One Teenager in Ten: Testimony by Gay and Lesbian Youth*. New York: Warner Books, 1986.

Howe, Louise Kapp. *Moments on Maple Avenue: The Reality of Abortion*. New York: Warner Books, 1986.

Muller, Ann. *Parents Matter: Parents' Relationships with Lesbian Daughters and Gay Sons*. Tallahassee, FL: Naiad Press, 1987.

REACH. *Some of the Nicest People I Know Have Herpes: The REACH Guide to Self-Help*. Research, Education and Assistance for Canadians with Herpes, P.O. Box 649, Station P, Toronto, Ontario M5S 2Y4.

Silverberg, Dr. Sy. *Lasting Longer*. Send $4.95 cheque or money order to Dr. Sy Silverberg, 526 Eglinton Avenue East, Toronto, Ontario M4I 1N6.

Suzuki, David, et al. *David Suzuki Talks About AIDS*. Toronto: General Publishing, 1987.